It Ends With You

Grow Up and Out of Dysfunction

By TINA B. TESSINA, PH.D.

Publisher: Muffinhaven Press
Long Beach, CA
United States of America
Copyright 2014 by Tina B. Tessina
All rights reserved
Printed in the United States of America by CreateSpace

ISBN:9781497330702

Original Edition: NEW PAGE BOOKS
A division of The Career Press, Inc.
Franklin Lakes, NJ

Copyright © 2003 by Tina B. Tessina, Ph.D.

IT ENDS WITH You
Illustrations in Chapter 6 by Riley K. Smith, MA

Order this title at http://www.tinatessina.com

Library of Congress Cataloging-in-Publication Data
Tessina, Tina B.
It ends with you : grow up and out of dysfunction *I* by Tina B. Tessina.
p. cm.
Includes index.
1. Adult children of dysfunctional families. 2. Problem families. 3. Adjustment (Psychology)
I. Title.

For my mother,
Anna Mae Stretch Bellocchio
1905—1999

Acknowledgments

To my husband, Richard Sharrard: Sweetheart, sharing life and love with you since 1982 has been a great joy. Thank you for all your love, your sense of humor, and your support and understanding.

To my dynamic agent and friend Laurie Harper, who has supported me through all the ups and downs of this crazy business of writing books. Thank you for all your advice, encouragement, and very practical help, and for friendship far beyond the role of an agent.

Yet another salute to my chosen family, in (more or less) alphabetical order: Isadora Alman and Morton Chalfy, Maggie and Ed Bialack, Victoria Bryan, Sylvia and Glen McWilliams, David Groves, Bobbi Palmer and Riley K. Smith. Each of you really knows what friends are for, and I am surrounded by love, laughter, and caring because of you. Thanks also to Cindy Cyr and the staff at The Coffee Cup, my writer's hangout.

Table of Contents

Introduction

Miracles do happen, but one has to work very hard for them.
— Chaim Weitzman

To grow up and out of a painful, dysfunctional past and all its leftovers—feelings, memories, pain, confusion, anger, fear, and persistent dysfunctional relationship patterns— may seem like a miracle, too wonderful to be possible. But it can be done, if you have the right tools and support. The purpose of this book is to lead you from the problems of the past into a satisfying, joyful, and successful future.

Most people tend to think of family legacies in terms of handed- down furniture, mementos, and money. But most of us actually get far larger inheritances of habits, attitudes, beliefs, and patterns. These old, learned ways of thinking and acting can create chaos in your life that resembles the upheaval of the past.

In nearly 40 years of psychotherapy practice, I have watched with awe as clients come to understand the power of childhood experience—how it can affect their lives without their knowledge. As they begin to understand and challenge their early learning, they gain the confidence and understanding they need to face the lessons of life on their own terms. Once they have unlocked their inner secrets, they are able to handle whatever surprises and challenges life holds and still see the humor, the beauty, and the joy of being alive. With the information and techniques in *It Ends with You,* you too can change your early programming and take charge of your life.

Whether your life feels good, just tolerable, overwhelming, or even miserable, until you explore the early learning that holds you back, a substantial amount of your personal energy can be tied up inside you. This bound energy has been unavailable to you for so long, you may not even realize it's missing, but your capacity to fully experience the joy of life, and a lot of your potential vitality, suffers.

There was a little girl
Who had a little curl
Right in the middle of her forehead.
And when she was good
She was very, very good
But when she was bad, she was horrid.

...goes the familiar nursery rhyme. Most of us know we either can be "very, very good" or "horrid," but seldom can we figure out why we act the way we do or the timing of either behavior.

If you can't trust yourself, whom can you trust? When you don't feel in control of your own reactions and emotions, how can you feel secure and competent? When a friend disappoints or betrays you or life hands you a difficult situation, such as illness, and you feel emotionally upset or out of control, what can you do about it?

We all have a need to feel in control and competent; our survival depends on it. We are naturally afraid of what we don't understand, what we feel we cannot control. When what feels uncontrollable is within ourselves, it becomes all the more threatening. Yet, most of us have at least some feelings or beliefs that seem too repulsive, primitive, dangerous, puzzling, unacceptable, embarrassing, and/or out of control to be safe.

But change, even for the better, can be frightening, too. Even as my clients agonize over how out of control they feel, and how remorseful they are about their history, they can fear and reject all suggestions and attempts to help them become more familiar with their hidden self and resist learning to manage their impulses and reactions more effectively. Many people seek hard and long for a way to avoid suppressed pain, shame, and guilt, to make it go away, to make everything "nice." Taken to an extreme, this avoidance is often the motivation and rationale behind drug use (from herbal remedies and Prozac to illegal street drugs), compulsions (if I get busy, obsessed, or overworked enough, I won't feel bad), and a desperate, panicky feeling of being out of control. It's very painful to feel hopeless and helpless about functioning well in life and in relationships.

Through my counseling practice, it soon became obvious that a large proportion of the problems adults have with life and relationships are a consequence of having grown up in a family with problems: divorce, alcoholism, rage, emotionally absent parents, or mental illness. Poor coping skills and inadequate decision-making are a natural consequence of growing up in such an environment, because most of what young children learn comes from observation and imitation.

What you learned before you were able to think abstractly, reason, and evaluate becomes embedded in your mind, but hidden out of your awareness. This creates mystery—you find yourself acting and thinking in ways that don't make sense to you. It's a frightening, out-of-control feeling, and many people panic and do destructive things to avoid being aware of it. Often, this panicky behavior replicates the dysfunctional behavior of ancestors. So, people who, as children, said, "I will never act like that," wind up behaving just as the person who troubled them most in childhood did. Others simply feel inadequate, as though someone else is in charge, or should be. Adults who have not examined the roots of their beliefs and behavior often find themselves acting in ways that do not produce good results in their grown-up lives and relationships. These people feel frustrated, mystified, and to a large degree out of control of themselves and their lives.

There is good news and bad news about fixing these problems in life. The good news is that early dysfunction can be healed, and therapy does work; there's even new research that says therapy can change brain chemistry. So what's the bad news? It's not easy, and it takes courage to do the work necessary.

Changing Your Beliefs and Behavior

This book is about understanding that growing up in a dysfunctional family can block you from realizing and using some of your finest natural gifts. *It Ends with You* will teach you, through exercises and information, how to open up, confront, and understand what has been hidden in you. You will come to understand the unique gifts you were born with, how they are blocked, how that blockage affects you today, and how unblocking these gifts will improve all your interactions—in business, friendship, and family.

It will help you examine not just the statistics that show that children of divorce can't keep their own marriages together, or children of alcoholics gravitate to dysfunctional partners, but *why* people have these problems, how they come to be, and, most important, what you can do to fix them.

In reading it, you'll learn:

➢ What dysfunction is

➢ How your family experiences shape you.

➢ Why you often feel out of control, or don't understand your own reactions.

➢ How to change your habits and belief systems to get the results you want.

Whatever your early family experience, whether the problems were mild or severe, you are not stuck with the result. Yes, your personality, beliefs, and habits were shaped in early childhood, before you knew what was influencing you. However, the good news is, you can change every bit of early "programming" that you wish to change and take control of your own life. In my counseling practice, I help clients do it every day. *It Ends with You* will take you through the same information, exercises, and guidelines I use with my clients. When you're done, you will know what you need to make your life your own.

Chapter 1: Dysfunctional Families and How They Grow

How children survive being Brought Up amazes me.

—Malcolm S. Forbes

What does it mean to grow up in a dysfunctional family? If you've followed pop psychology, been in a 12-step program, such as Alcoholics Anonymous or Adult Children of Alcoholics, watched *Oprah* or *Dr. Phil,* read books and magazines, you've probably seen or heard the term *dysfunctional* many times, and may even have an idea that it means a messed-up family with problems. Perhaps the word has come to mean that the family experienced violence, various kinds of abuse, or alcohol and drug abuse. Certainly, all these things can be included in the definition of *dysfunctional family.* But, to psychologists, dysfunction has a specific meaning, and the manifestation in families isn't always so obvious or dramatic.

Function of a Family

Ideally, a family has a *function:* that is, a job to do. A healthy family should create and sustain an environment that promotes emotional and physical health and psychological well-being for its members. To fulfill this function, families should know how to nurture, support, encourage, protect, teach, create boundaries and structure, and work together as a team.

According to recovery expert John Bradshaw in *Bradshaw on the Family:*

THE FUNCTIONAL FAMILY stands for

F ills its function

U nderstands everyone's purpose

N urtures—everyone's needs are met

C ommunicates frequently and effectively

T eaches the children what they need to know

I ntimacy is available

O pen to new ideas

N ever punishes by shaming or withholding love

A lways seeks to understand each other

L OVE IS MOST IMPORTANT (including, sometimes, tough love)

F ights fair

A ssists each other (teamwork)

M akes each individual important

I n times of trouble, focuses on solving the problem, support

L ets each member be an individual

Y OU have the power to be functional, no matter what anyone else is doing

Of course, it is much easier for psychologists and recovery experts to preach about functional families than it is for ordinary people to create a working, healthy family. Often, parents have little or no training in how to establish a healthy relationship with each other, even before they begin to take on the enormous responsibility of raising children. These parents are products of their own parents' lack of information, and the cycle of ignorance and incompetence may go back many generations. Psychologists and psychotherapists know that family dysfunction is a problem with a long history. Families pass their habits, personality traits, and traditions down, generation after generation. We acknowledge this when we say a child has "his grandfather's sense of humor" or "her grandmother's sweet disposition." A mom might say, "He has my brother's bad temper," or a dad opine, "Susie is moody, like my mother."

"Families repeat themselves within and across generations," writes Northwestern University professor Kathleen Galvin. "Members become caught up in predictable but often unexamined life patterns which arc created, in part, through their interactions with others." How do these family characteristics, habits, and attributes get passed down?

Early Imprinting

Even before we're born, we begin learning about love and family. Research shows that babies learn to recognize familiar voices and respond to emotions and time schedules even while still in the womb. Babies are born totally focused on the familiar voices, heartbeats, and body scents they learned to recognize while in the womb. At birth, we are already relating to the other family members who surround us—parents, siblings, and extended family members. Before we know who we are as individuals, we learn how to be a part of the family. Before we have the ability to evaluate and reason, we uncritically absorb everything that happens around us. As infant brain cells develop, they are influenced by the family environment, and our emotional responses are learned there. Whether the family is happy and healthy, cold and withdrawn, violent and hostile, or (like most families) somewhere in between, as small children, we .don't question whether it is right or wrong. Whatever goes on behind the doors of home is what a child accepts as "the way it is."

Children learn from observation and imitation. Before the age of 5, when a child begins to develop the ability to think objectively and abstractly, each child is a very impressionable observer of the world around him, which consists mostly of family. The naive child accepts that whatever goes on within the family is "normal"—or rather, he really doesn't understand that anything else exists.

The most poignant and unforgettable example of this I ever saw was a local newspaper article about a little boy who was taken from his family by Child Protective Services for neglect and abuse. His family was charged with abusing him by keeping him in a coffin- sized box, and only allowing him out for brief periods, such as for meals. The boy was routinely taken to a group home while the case was being investigated. When the boy was introduced to the other children in the home, he wanted to know where their boxes were. He had nothing to use as a comparison, so he believed all children would have the same experience.

Family Rules

Each child struggles to find a way to succeed in the family environment. Perhaps the unspoken (but easily observable in action) rules in the family say that the angriest person gets what he wants, or the person who suffers most gets the attention, or the family member who is the least demanding gets praised. These "rules" can vary widely from family to family. Perhaps there is one "golden child" who gets all the attention and perks, or perhaps the boys are favored, having to do little, while the girls do all the chores. In some families, one child is designated the "smart one," while another is the "pretty one," or the "clumsy," "stupid," or "hopeless" one. Children in such environments soon learn that they will be cast in these roles anyway, so they find ways to take advantage of whatever benefits they can find. If you're the "clumsy" child, and you get a lot of attention and sympathy for being awkward, it's almost impossible to resist the expectations that you'll stumble and knock things over. Before long, you begin to believe the designation is true. In my work supervising counseling interns for a center that deals with many children and families referred by the court or school, these unspoken rules become obvious very quickly.

These pressures distort the child's view of himself, and also his social interactions, and even his understanding of what love, communication, and emotions are. These apparent "truths" and ways of surviving or succeeding in the environment are learned at a very deep, subconscious level, and remain with us into adulthood.

To illustrate generational heritage, family systems expert and psychotherapist Virginia Satir used the following story in her workshops and her book *Peoplemaking:*

Once a woman was preparing dinner, and her husband, watching, asked,

"Why do you cut the ends off the ham before you bake it?"
"My mother always did it this way."
He knew better than to comment further, but he one day asked his mother-in-law. "Why do you cut the ends off the ham before you bake it?"
"My mother always did it this way."

Luckily, the grandmother was still living, so he had a chance to ask her:
"Why do you cut the ends off the ham before you bake it?"
"My roasting pan is too small."

Silly as it may sound, many family traditions and interactions are passed on in just this way. Grandparents or parents may have had a good reason for their actions, but the children, not knowing the reason, are imprinted with the behavior and dutifully follow through, without examining whether that tradition is appropriate to current conditions. For example, when one generation is traumatized by an apocalyptic event, such as the Holocaust in Germany, Poland, and surrounding areas; the killing fields of the Khmer Rouge in Cambodia; the communist takeover of China; pre-Civil War slavery and postwar segregation of African-Americans; or the Great Depression in America, the results of their trauma can be seen in their children and even their grandchildren. Fear of authority figures (such as soldiers or police) may be passed down for generations, even though the grandchildren of the traumatized individuals have had no negative experiences with people in uniform. Penny-pinching and food-hoarding, for example, may become a family trait for a family that endured harsh poverty during the Depression, and could persist even after that family becomes financially very comfortable.

Other trauma gets passed down, also. Studies of prisoners incarcerated for violent crimes show that an overwhelming percentage of them experienced violence in childhood. Whenever I work with clients who are survivors of abuse, checking into the past reveals that the abusive parent or grandparent was abused, or witnessed abuse, in his or her own past. Alcoholism is often a multigenerational family trait. The same holds true with sexual trauma, such as molestation or incest. These problems are passed down in the family in much the same way that cooking styles and holiday celebrations become traditions. Whether functional or dysfunctional, the behavior, attitudes, and communication styles of the parents are passed down to the children.

Blame Is Not Necessary

Most of my clients do not want to spend time blaming their parents for problems they have in their lives. Many of them feel protective toward their parents, who often struggled to make it through each day. We do not look at dysfunctional patterns in order to blame anyone, but to better understand our often inexplicable reactions and habits. Knowing where we learned certain behaviors, how they worked, and the beliefs we developed as children in the dysfunctional atmosphere can make it much easier to change and correct problem thinking and behavior.

When clients are struggling to understand how they can identify the mistakes their parents made without blaming the parents, I use the following metaphor—deadly ignorance:

At the turn of the century, before much was known about bacteria and viruses; many children died of diphtheria, a deadly disease frequently borne in contaminated water. Parents could easily have given their children the water that was fatal to them, without knowing. In this case, we needn't blame the parents, but the ignorance, for the damage to the children.

Family dysfunction is similar. Parents are often ignorant of the damage they're inflicting on children through criticism, severe punishment, or neglect. In most cases, my clients' abusive and neglectful parents were treating their children better than they had been treated themselves.

Child and spousal abuse is nothing new. Readers of history know that until relatively recently, violence, rape, and incest were acceptable (at the least overlooked, but often encouraged) within families. As with slavery, marriage and parenthood were social institutions that gave some people absolute power over others. Until we acknowledge that fact, and the related fact that we are changing our definitions of acceptable family behavior, we will never fully understand the cycles of incest and violence that we are now attempting to break.

Modern terminology often ignores these facts. Words such as:

> **Perpetrator:** seen as the "criminal"—the one who commits the act. This does not acknowledge that almost every perpetrator is also an abuse survivor.

> **Dysfunctional Families:** seen as "bad parents"—familial groupings struggling with addiction, violence and unhealthy relationship dynamics. The struggle of the adults involved to overcome their own abusive histories is often not recognized.

> **Adult Survivors of Incest/Abuse:** seen as "the victim"— the abused child, now grown up. His or her powerlessness and

unconscious participation in the family dysfunction is either excused or condemned, when it could be explored as a basis for learning.

➤ **Adult Children of Dysfunctional Families:** also seen as "victims," and the only group being encouraged to redefine the family in healthier terms. Most ACDFs don't understand the social revolution that's necessary to truly heal and redefine the family process.

In a society that wants to point fingers at a "villain," pity the "victim" and insist on "instant solutions," it is easier to call abuse and incest "criminal acts" and put all our energy on finding and punishing the perpetrator than to take an honest look at the social values and historical dynamics that create both villain and victim. It is easier for the survivors of dysfunction and abuse to blame those who were supposed to be in charge than it is to look at their own patterns, take responsibility, and correct them.
To effectively solve the problems, we must see:

➤ The denial and secrecy that result by shaming and victimizing survivors to such an extent that they "forget" they were abused and live mystified, pain-filled lives, until one day their devastating memories suddenly erupt.

➤ The pain and terror of "perpetrators" who feel out of control, worthless, and desperate enough to "act out" what they cannot heal or often even remember.

➤ The helplessness and confusion of families who are living the only lives they know, blindly re-enacting history or fearfully repressing feelings, and unconsciously maiming themselves and their children in the process.

➤ Guilt is paralyzing, so when we insist on placing blame, we ensure the perpetuation of the very problem we so despise.

Is the situation hopeless, then? Are we doomed to repeat history forever? Not if we learn from it. What relief there is in realizing that we've not just sunk to new depths, but we're just dragging ourselves out of the mire of the past! How much easier it is for perpetrators and survivors alike to find the energy to learn new behavior and heal old wounds when they recognize the long history of the problems. Becoming aware that the cycle has been self-perpetuating, with variations, for centuries, handed down from great-grandparent, to grandparent, to parent, to child empowers us to do the dual work of breaking the old cycle and simultaneously healing old wounds and learning not to pass them on.

"Memories, good or bad," wrote socially conscious psychiatrist Thomas Szasz in *Heresies,* "cannot be removed as if they were art objects or useless pieces of junk...the way to forget X is by learning Y, and the way to achieve superior skill in forgetting (what one wants to forget) is not by practicing the art of forgetting (since there is no such art), but by practicing the art of learning." To expunge the old, destructive behavior we must learn the truth:

> ➢ Child and spousal abuse and incest is not new, but handed down from generation to generation.

> ➢ In the continuous abuse cycle, it is not possible to distinguish victims from perpetrators—the abused of one generation is the abuser of the next.

> ➢ Only education and information, including specific instruction about healthy family intimacy, will heal the problem.

> ➢ To heal, it is necessary to face the truth, which is usually preserved in old, repressed feelings. Releasing and acknowledging the old feelings creates room for new learning.

And so it goes. There is no doubt that we are influenced, and that sometimes the events that shaped us are mindlessly repeated despite circumstances that have changed.

Perception and personality are also influential. One child may feel defeated and helpless in response to the same event that energizes and mobilizes a brother or sister. A granddaughter may feel accepted and supported by her grandmother, though the girl's mother always felt rejected and misunderstood by the very same woman.

The task for all of us is to rise above the issues and wounds of childhood. Becoming truly adult, autonomous, and able to govern ourselves and our responses to those around us:

> We can use our inbred gifts of intelligence and spirit to spell out new ways of relating to those who cannot effectively relate to us.

> We can work together to change what was to what might have been.

> We can become self-nurtured enough to be truly charitable.

> We can learn to give without requiring return.

To accomplish this, it is necessary to identify and understand what dysfunction (whether severe or mild) was present in your childhood, to decide to take responsibility for your life now, and to resolve old pain and change old ideas and behaviors. The purpose of this book is to show you how to accomplish all of this and reclaim your life.

Identifying Dysfunction

So, how do you identify the dysfunction in your early family? In therapy, we often use a tool called a *genogram,* which is a map of the behaviors, strengths, weaknesses, and problems in your family. Genograms are used by therapists, researchers, and clients to better understand the history and patterns of the family. Standard genograms can be quite complicated, using various symbols, such as squares for men and circles for women, and indicating relationship connections with dotted, single, or double lines to indicate whether the people are distant, close, or enmeshed, and jagged lines to indicate abusive connections.

In the following exercise, I have simplified the genogram process to help you create a simplified map of your own family history, which you can use to identify both your own behaviors and also the kinds of people you tend to choose for relationships.

EXERCISE

Mapping Your Family

You'll need a pen or black marker, a pad of regular lined paper, a large board or piece of newsprint or butcher paper, and some colored markers.

1. On the pad, make a list of the names of every member of your family, going back to your great-grandparents if possible. Once your list is made, organize it in rows on the larger paper, with plenty of space between each name, like this:

GEN 1	Great-grandmother	Great-grandfather	Great-grandmother	Great-grandfather
GEN 2	Great Aunt	Grandmother	Grandfather	Great Uncle
GEN 3	Aunt Uncle	Mother Father	Aunt Uncle	
GEN 4	Cousin Cousin	Sister Yourself	Brother Cousin	Cousin

2. Once you have included everyone you know in your family on your chart, write characteristics of each person under his or her name. Include good and bad traits. For example, under "Father" you might write: sense of humor, hard worker, smoker, bad temper, overweight, overbearing, loving. Include such problems as abusive, vain, intelligent, alcoholic, money problems, workaholic, unfaithful, or dishonest where they fit.

3. Using colored markers, underline the traits you like in whatever color you like best, and underline the traits you don't like in another color.

When you're done, put your chart away for at least a day. After a break from it, take it out again and take a fresh look at it.

Analysis: How Much Dysfunction?

4. Do you see recurring traits in family members? Draw a circle around those traits.

5. Can you follow any traits down through the generations? If so, draw lines connecting them.

6. Identify which traits have passed down to you, and draw a circle around them in a different color.

When you have completed this analysis, you'll have a sense of how much function and/or dysfunction exists in your family, how far back it goes (although it undoubtedly extends back farther than this chart), and how it has passed down to you.

Your family legacy may seem overwhelming when you first look at it, but you'll find, as you read through the rest of the book, that this information is exactly what you need to begin the process of changing yourself and reclaiming your life. Armed with this knowledge, you can free yourself from whatever part of your family patterns you wish, and create the life and the relationships you want. The power is yours.

If, in the course of doing the previous exercise, you realize you have intense feelings toward one or several of your family members, you may want to do the following exercise to express and clear up some of those feelings.

EXERCISE

Love Letter

Writing has a powerful effect on your emotional state. The following exercise is designed to help you fully express feelings that may have lain dormant for a long time, or may be too intense and jumbled for your to process effectively. You'll find it helpful in expressing what you feel, especially if you're having difficulty letting go, forgiving, grieving for, or being appropriately angry at someone.

Important: This letter is not designed to be mailed to anyone.

After you write it, you may decide to write another letter appropriately adjusted for the other person to read. The point of this exercise is to let your feelings out, uncensored and unedited. Begin by expressing your anger, resentment, and blame, and allow yourself to move through the other levels until you get down to the love.

You may find that your feelings begin pouring out as you write. If so, just go with what you feel. If you get stuck or confused, using the following suggested lead-in phrases may help you.

1. Anger and blame
I don't like it when...
I resent...
I hate it when...
I'm fed up with...
I'm tired of...

2. Hurt and sadness
I feel sad when...
I feel hurt because...
I feel awful because...
I feel disappointed because...

3. Fear and insecurity
I feel afraid...
I'm afraid that...
I feel scared because...
I don't understand...

4. Guilt and responsibility
I'm sorry that...
I'm sorry for...
Please forgive me for...
I didn't mean to...

5. Love, forgiveness, understanding, and desire
I love you because...
I love when...
Thank you for...
I understand that...
I forgive you for...
I want...

If, as you write this letter, you find that memories of previously suppressed traumatic events arise, you may need to get some help from a counselor or therapist. Detailed instructions for how to find an appropriate counselor are in Chapter 5.

Viewing the dysfunction in your family so clearly may be uncomfortable and may bring up anger or sadness. Don't let it discourage you. You have just begun a discovery process that will allow you to grow out of the dysfunction and create the life you want.

Chapter 2: What You Might Have Learned in Childhood

Children have more need of models than of critics.
—Joseph Joubert (1754—1824)

Because, as children, we learn so much by experience and emulation, our early family experience has a huge influence on our beliefs, habits, and values that can affect us for the rest of our lives. "Poor health begins early in life, as does good health," said Rena Repetti, associate professor of psychology at UCLA, in the March 2002 issue of the journal *Psychological Bulletin.* "Growing up in risky families creates a cascade of risk, beginning early in life, which puts a child not only at immediate risk, but also at long-term and lifelong risk for a wide variety of physical and mental health ailments."

Early Learning

Research in developmental learning shows that children younger than about 5 years old learn in three major ways: imitation, interaction, and sensory experience. Because their brains are still developing, and they have little life experience to draw on, young children are not yet capable of abstract thinking and reasoning. Experts in early childhood psychological development, beginning with Jean Piaget and Erik Erikson maintain that abstract, rational thinking only begins developing about at age 5 and is not fully present until about age 8, when they begin to ask questions about things they cannot directly experience, such as what death is, how electricity works, where you go when you go out to work, or what God looks like.

"From the time of conception to the first day of kindergarten, development proceeds at a pace exceeding that of any subsequent stage of life," write scientists of the National Research Council in *From Neurons to Neighborhoods.* "What happens during the first months and years of life matters a lot...."

Before abstract thinking develops, children learn from experience and the senses and do not have the ability to evaluate their experience logically. Young children cannot clearly grasp what they cannot physically experience, or understand through the senses, so they make connections between things that may not actually relate. That's why they'll believe almost anything they're told by an adult, such as fairy tales and the existence of Santa Claus, and they don't question illogical cause-and-effect connections such as "step on a crack, break your mother's back." Psychologists call the kind of thinking young children use *magical thinking.*

In *The Real 13th Step,* I described it this way:

> Children, wide-eyed, believe that the Tooth Fairy really left the quarter, or that Mommy's kiss heals a bumped knee, or that the Santa in the department store is really going to bring the toy they ask for down the chimney on Christmas Eve. Small children love to play peekaboo, because they believe they can't be seen when *their* eyes are covered up.

Children cannot see the cause-and-effect connection between events (a small child cannot understand that planting a seed will produce tomatoes weeks later); they think in very concrete ways, and they cannot understand abstract concepts (such as *near and far,* and *left and right)* until after about the age of 5. They are the center of their tiny universe, they believe everything that happens relates to them, and they perceive their behavior to be the cause of every event. (When Mommy smiles or. frowns, baby feels responsible.)

Connecting unrelated events and behavior in this way is what psychologists' term *magical thinking,* the stage in a child's thinking in which we believe we are the cause of physical phenomena. In *Imaginary Crimes,* psychologists Lewis Engel and Tom Ferguson show that magical thinking begins as part of normal childhood development: "As children we are ignorant of the laws of cause and effect, and may at times come to irrational conclusions...Magical thinking is the child's belief that she has the ability to make things happen by simply thinking about them."

In the film *Home Alone,* when the young hero awakens to find himself alone in the house, he (falsely, but naturally for his 7 years of age) concludes it's because the night before he wished his whole family would disappear. The more prosaic truth, that he's been accidentally forgotten by his rather disorganized family amid the chaos of leaving for vacation, simply doesn't occur to him. It is this quality of childhood thinking that makes fairy tales, fables, and magical stories so believable to children. In their eyes, they are as real as many other "unseen" events: Daddy's work, older brother's school, germs, "when you grow up." If a child cannot experience something with her own five senses, it is not real to her, and seems like magic.

"Magic is the belief that certain words, gestures or behaviors can change reality. Dysfunctional parents often reinforce their children's magical thinking," writes John Bradshaw in *New Realities* magazine (July/August 1990). "It's natural for a child to think magically. But if a child is wounded through unmet dependency needs, he does not really grow up. The adult he becomes is still contaminated by the magical thinking of a child."

Very young children learn with less mental capacity, less understanding, and a less functional brain than adults. Their brains are still developing. According to Dr. Arthur Janov, in *The Biology of Love,*

"The forces driving our behavior are located largely in three different brain systems:

1. The cortex, which operates conscious-awareness.

2. The limbic system, which drives feeling.

3. The brainstem, which processes instincts and survival functions.

Imprints take place in different parts of the brain depending on their force and when they occurred. Very early developments, rebirth and birth, will impact the most competent nervous system at the time—the brainstem. Traumas in early childhood will affect the brainstem and limbic system. Later, as the Neocortex develops, thinking processes will be involved."

Because they are not yet able to grasp logical explanations and teachings, young children learn in three major ways:

1. Imitation

2. Interaction

3. Sensory experience

Imitation

Young children learn by imitating what the grown-ups around them do and say. Recently, a friend told me about her 2 1/2-year-old granddaughter who, while in the bathtub, said, "Holy Smoke! There's sure a lot of bubbles here!" Of course, we all laughed - because this very young child sounded so adult. Recently, one of my clients was recalling "playing house" with her little sister. She laughed when she said, "Whichever one of us played

'Mommy' tied a diaper around her head - because my mother was always lying down with a cold pack because of her migraines." Children don't understand the fine points, and these two had decided that being Mommy meant having a headache. Would it be surprising if one or both of them had migraines later in life?

So much of what young children learn is learned in this imitative way, without fully understanding the reason behind the event. This is a major cause of "family traits," such as gestures, facial expressions, and oft-quoted phrases. We imitate our other family members from such an early age that by the time we're adults, many shared traits and mannerisms come naturally, and are often evident to others who know us.

Interaction

Small children are so focused on non-verbal interaction that they are very sensitive to the responses and reactions of the people around them. As a child relates to others in the family circle, he or she quickly learns to judge what behaviors are acceptable and unacceptable by observing the emotional reactions and physical responses of others to his or her own behavior.

Research shows that young babies take most of their clues from their mother's responses. In filmed experiments with babies a few months old, mothers were asked not to respond to their babies for a few minutes and to keep a deadpan expression. The babies begin contented and comfortable, but when mothers stop responding, baby first begins trying harder to get a response, then becomes visibly anxious, and then dissolves in tears. All this happens in less than five minutes.

With this kind of sensitivity, and such an intense focus on the response of family members, young children quickly learn to act in the ways that "work" (get a response). If families don't react unless a baby cries, he or she will tend to cry more; or if giggles and smiles get a lot of attention, a baby will tend to smile more.

"When there is little emotional rapport between mother and newborn," writes Dr. Arthur Janov, in the book *The Biology of Love*, "nerve cells in certain brain structures do not develop properly. The prefrontal cortex— the planning, thinking, logical, integrating outer layer of brain cells—is impaired by a lack of early love and will not function to full capacity later in life. The deprivation leads to less control over one's impulses and a reduced ability to think abstractly, as well as impaired coordination and a diminished ability to plan ahead...When a father never touches his infant, is impatient and angry, and demands obedience from a 2-year-old, the frontal cortical neurons are going to be deficient...for a very long time. Hugs and kisses during these critical periods make those neurons grow and connect properly with other neurons. You can kiss that brain into maturity. A father who never shows happiness to see that baby, never responds with kindness to her cries is forming a new brain in the offspring."

In this way, our behavior is shaped, for good or ill, by the responses we get in the first few years of our lives. By the time we understand behavior and interaction, we have already developed deep-seated habits we didn't choose.

Sensory Experience

Young children try to put everything and anything into their mouths. They grab at shiny or bright objects, and they react to sudden noise, familiar voices, and music. Even very young children will sway or bounce to music, and recognize the sound of Mommy's or Daddy's voice. Touching, feeling, smelling, hearing and tasting are the toddlers' ways to experience and attempt to understand whatever he or she encounters. Babies react to the way it feels to be held, which is why a baby will be fussy in the arms of someone who is nervous about holding her and will immediately calm down when an experienced person picks her up, even if the experienced person isn't Mom.

For example, Judith, who raised three children, was visiting her daughter Melissa and brand-new grandson. The baby was fussy, and the new mom was getting more and more anxious while trying to calm him. The more anxious the new mother got, the more the baby cried and struggled. Grandma reached out her hands, took the little boy, and, in a couple of minutes, had him calmed down and falling asleep. Stunned, Melissa looked at Judith and demanded, "How did you do that?" Her mother couldn't really explain, but with her help, Melissa quickly learned to handle the baby calmly and confidently, and he stopped being so fussy. (This is one reason that it is so valuable to new mothers to be surrounded by more experienced women. Much of this non-verbal interaction and sensory input can only be learned by experience and mentoring.)

Your Buried Mind

Imitation, interaction, and sensory experience are learning methods of the *limbic brain*. Once the frontal cortex develops, this early learning is buried.

The attitudes, beliefs, models, emotional responses, and skills formed in early childhood lie so deeply buried that they are very difficult to change or unlearn. It's as if there are two different aspects of you: the rational grown-up and the immature child. Rational thinking is the process adults are supposed to use, and childlike thinking belongs to the period long before your earliest memories began. Therefore, it is difficult as an adult to become aware of or understand many of our emotional reactions and responses. The early part of your brain still perceives and thinks about the world magically while you tend to think and communicate like an adult.

You may never have understood why you felt so helplessly unable to control yourself at certain times or why you can overreact to small problems, exacerbating the risk and pain. You might have overwhelming feelings of anxiety, depression, or helplessness, or you may even feel numb. There may be behaviors you don't seem to be able to conquer, such as smoking, overspending, overeating, or overreacting. You may have struggled to change, yet failed over and over again.

As an adult, you may know that you are a worthwhile person who doesn't need to depend on others for support and guidance. But your early experience is buried so deep and thinks so differently that you wind up saying, "I know I shouldn't (or should) do it, but I just can't help myself."

Those children lucky enough to be born into a functional, extended family, with parents who are never overloaded or stressed, and who have the education and skill to know how to meet the needs of their offspring, may have everything they need to function effectively in life. For most children, though, the circumstances and stresses of their early years leave a lasting legacy of stress, struggle, and insecurity. The biggest problem is that the information, habits, and beliefs you acquired in childhood are buried. As an adult, you feel uncomfortable, insecure, anxious, depressed, overwhelmed, or inadequate, but you don't understand why.

As an adult, you do not outgrow your original dependent childhood personality or old, negative judgments about your ability to cope with life effectively. Instead, your childhood mind underlies your adult mind. These early attitudes can make your subsequent attempts at independence and self-control difficult, your childhood personality (which many psychologists call the *inner child* or the *subconscious)* becomes a shadow self, erupting at inopportune times and giving you the impression that you are unable to manage life on your own.

The minute you get stressed, overloaded, or confused, your child mind reasserts itself and takes over, causing you to revert to old, familiar modes of behavior. For example, you might have decided to get in charge of your anxiety or anger, because you realize, rationally, that it creates problems. Logically, you know how to act appropriately, and what self-control is, but your spouse annoys you, or your child rebels, and suddenly you're too upset to think rationally about it. Instead, you react out of the emotional, childlike part of your brain, and get angry or you panic again. You never get a chance to think rationally before you act out your fear or frustration.

Discovering What You Learned

The problem with what we learn in childhood is that it stays with us, and it remains below awareness until it erupts. And because such emotional outbursts and reactions feel foreign to the "self" with which we identify, they can be quickly denied or forgotten. Dramatic overreactions don't feel familiar, so it's tempting to deny that they're real. However, as long as they're overlooked, they will be a problem in your life, disrupting relationships, sabotaging your goals, and creating unnecessary stress.

So, how can you become aware of what you learned then that's still affecting you today? Awareness and acceptance are the keys to understanding this hidden part of your personality.

Self-Awareness

Awareness of self comes from simply paying attention to your thoughts, feelings, and reactions. Becoming self-aware is seeking to understand what you feel, how much of it is related to the present moment, current events, your physical state, and how much is related to your personal history.

Caring about what you feel is not being self-centered or narcissistic. In fact, a clinically narcissistic person doesn't know what he or she truly feels and doesn't care about his own feelings or the feelings of others. Caring about what you feel and knowing more about it actually makes you more compassionate, empathetic, and caring toward others. Awareness and understanding of your own feelings also means you'll be much more intelligent about others' feelings—that is, you'll have the wisdom of your own feelings to help you sort out when others' feelings are real or deceptive.

EXERCISE

Developing Self-Awareness

You can become more self-aware in this moment, as you read this book.

1. Begin with your sensory experience.

> **Sight:** Look around—where are you? Are you sitting at home, in your most comfortable chair? Lying on the couch? Are you at the beach, in the library, riding a bus, or taking a break at work? What are your surroundings? Is it night or day? Are you reading by natural or artificial light? Look at the whiteness of the pages, the black type, the colors of the book cover. Look at everything around you, and notice the colors, shapes, and textures.

> **Touch:** Is your seat comfortable? How does your body feel right now? Are you relaxed or cramped in an uncomfortable position? Are you tired or well-rested? How does the book feel in your hand? What other body sensations are you having? Are you reading on a moving vehicle, such as a bus, plane, or train? Are you hungry, or are you full from just having eaten? Are you alert or sleepy? Are you warm enough? Feel all of your body, inside and out, and notice all the physical sensations. Feel your breathing, in and out.

> **Sound:** Are you reading in a quiet place? Can you hear your own heartbeat and breathing? Is there music playing? Are you blocking out noise? Are people talking around you? Is a clock ticking? Can you hear phones or distant traffic?

> **Smell and Taste**: Are you drinking or eating something while you read? Can you taste coffee, water, a soft drink? Pick up the book or the reader and smell it. Can you smell the paper and ink or the screen? Can you smell dust or fumes in the air around you? Can you taste the air? How does your own mouth taste to you?

2. Now, notice your feelings. Are you anxious, tense, or worried about something? Are you calm? Focus on your breathing and feel the body sensations that go with it— the cool air coming in, the rhythm of your lungs expanding and deflating. If you pay attention to your breathing for a little while, it helps you be more aware of your feelings. Are you reacting emotionally to your surroundings? If it's noisy, are you annoyed? If it's too

quiet, are you uneasy? If you're warm and comfy, do you feel peaceful and soothed? It's usually easier to feel feelings if you give them a little time to rise to the surface and if you're in a place where you won't be disturbed, but they are moving through you every moment of every day. When you take the time to notice them, you can often use that information to help you handle situations wisely.

3. Whether you realize it or not, there is a lot of chatter going on in your mind. At this moment, you may be arguing or agreeing with what you're reading, or commenting on whether you think this exercise is helpful, or criticizing or worrying about whether you're doing it correctly. Bits of songs, movie or TV dialogue, or conversations from other times and places may be running by like a background soundtrack. Sit and listen for a few moments, and try to identify each thought that goes by. Do you hear someone's voice, or several people? *Don't worry, this is not a hallucination— hallucinations are auditory—they sound as if someone is actually in the room speaking to you. The "voices" we all have in our heads are like recordings of things we actually heard, being played back on an endless loop.* With a little practice, you'll become aware of a "soundtrack" composed of memories, thoughts, criticisms, background noise, TV, music, movies, the news, and other noises you've recorded in your lifetime.

As simple as this exercise seems, if you do it repeatedly throughout your days, you'll find that your self-knowledge grows rapidly. After a few weeks, you'll be much more aware of your own body, your feelings, and your thoughts. Once aware, you have a chance to manage and/or change them to be more effective for you, as we'll see later in this book. Accurate awareness of your thoughts, feelings, and actions is the key to getting in charge of your life and changing it into the life you want to live. But if it is not accompanied by gentle self-acceptance, self-awareness can be too painful.

Self-Acceptance

If you use your newfound awareness to criticize everything you say, feel, think, or do, it will become a source of discomfort. Many of my clients have trouble with the idea of being accepting of themselves because they believe it will lead to being egotistical, conceited, and self-centered. Or worse, that it will lead to being self-satisfied and not improving. The key to self-awareness that is appropriate and effective is self-acceptance.

Self-acceptance is not the same as self-indulgence. Accepting who you are means deciding to be supportive of yourself and also realistic about being a human. You can learn to be accepting of your own faults and mistakes with kindness, as you would with a friend, without giving up any of your desire to improve. In fact, the honesty of self- awareness, coupled with self-acceptance and kindness to yourself *increases* the likelihood that you will be motivated to become a better person.

EXERCISE

The following exercise will help you learn to treat yourself with more acceptance and kindness. You will need a pen or pencil and a notebook, journa4 or writing paper.

Learning Self-Acceptance

1. *Observe how you relate to yourself:* Do you treat yourself the way you would like to treat others? Do you treat yourself the way you would like your friends to treat you? Would you be willing to be friends with someone who treated you the way you treat yourself? Do you honor what you think and feel as you would honor a friend's opinions? Do you take the time to ask your own opinion of what you are doing, or do you just focus on what other people think?

2. *Would you consider yourself a good friend?* You may be dismayed to find out how very differently you treat yourself from the way you would treat a friend. Perhaps you don't keep your promises to yourself as you would those to a friend. You might not treat yourself with kindness and respect. Maybe you mentally nag or criticize yourself. Although you never break a date with a friend, you may keep putting off your time with yourself or avoid caring for yourself with exercise or relaxation. The best test of your friendship with

yourself is to ask: If someone else treated you the way you treat yourself, would you want to be his or her friend?

3. *Reevaluate your internal friendship:* Once you have compared the way you treat yourself to the way you relate to friends, you have some more thinking to do and some choices to make. First, decide how you want to improve the way you treat yourself. Develop three simple ways you can be a better friend to yourself. One way to do this, if you have a friend you feel good about, is to treat yourself as you would treat the other person. Ask yourself, "How would I respond to Maggie in a similar situation?" Chances are, you will find you are usually kinder to her than to yourself. How would you speak to your friend if you thought she forgot to do something? Now, do you treat yourself more harshly? By comparing the way you treat yourself with the way you treat your friends, you will begin to develop clear guidelines about how to change the way you treat yourself. Write down your ideas about befriending yourself.

4. *Practice to develop the habit:* Once you begin changing the way you treat yourself, you must be consistent in order to develop a habit of being nice to yourself. Just as you learn to become friends with others because they consistently treat you well, you can build a friendship with yourself by consistently treating yourself as you would a friend. Once you develop your ideas about how to be a better friend to yourself, post your list of guidelines somewhere visible. Renew your plan for being a better friend to yourself every week for at least six weeks. At the end of that time, you'll find that treating yourself well becomes much easier and feels more comfortable. In short, you will be building self-acceptance.

Your Family Legacy

Now that you have increased your awareness of your personal traits and feelings and how you treat yourself, it's time to examine where you acquired these tendencies. Using your self-awareness, begin with the evidence. Do you notice that you overreact to certain situations? Do your children, your friends, your partner, or your family ever mention that you're getting too upset or responding inappropriately? Under stress, do you find yourself saying or doing things that feel as if someone else is making the responses? Let's use the genogram from Chapter 1 to examine the beliefs, habits, emotional reactions, and attitudes you may have acquired from family members through imitation and observation in your childhood.

EXERCISE
Building Blocks

This is a guided meditation. You may find it helpful to record the following directions on tape and play them back for yourself or have a friend read them aloud.

1. Using the genogram from Chapter 1, pick the two people from your family (usually parents) who seem most powerful or influential in your childhood. Take a moment to think of each person and remember how he or she seemed to you when you were a child. What was important about each person? What did you like or not like about them? What were their positive and negative personality traits?

2. Sit quietly and comfortably, close your eyes, and picture these two people standing side by side. Now picture a pile of bricks or building blocks in front of each of them.

3. Concentrate on the first person, perhaps your mother, and label each of the blocks with a personality trait or habit. For example, in front of Mother, the pile of blocks may include: physically affectionate, smiles a lot, nags, wonderful cook, worries, helpful, supportive, overeater, poor self-esteem, moody, talks too much. Continue to fill in the blocks until you have captured all the positive and negative traits you think are important.

4. Then move on to the second person, perhaps your father, and fill in his blocks, which might include: rough, backslapping sense of humor, teases

and jokes, perfectionist, reliable, shows love with money, good provider, honest, heavy smoker, disciplinarian, critical, swears a lot.

5. Once you have the blocks labeled, let the people recede into the background, and focus now on the blocks. Sort them into two piles: those qualities you like and want to keep for yourself, and those qualities you do not want to carry on. Take your time, as this is an important choice.

6. When you finish sorting, look at the pile of qualities you want to keep. Is it complete? What does it need? That is, what are the qualities not on any of the blocks, but that you would like to cultivate in yourself?

7. Create new blocks from other people on the genogram or other people you know today. If no one in your family or among your friends possessed the trait, look for examples among fictional characters, public personalities, teachers, or other role models.

8. Add the admirable qualities of these people to your "keeps" pile. Put the "keeps" pile in a safe place, where you can get at it whenever you need to.

9. Now get rid of the pile of traits you don't want. You may want to leave it with the original owners, burn it, or put it in the trash.

10. Bring your chosen models back into the foreground and thank them for their help, their examples, both good and bad, and anything else you wish to thank them for, then say good-bye and come back to everyday reality by opening your eyes.

11. Make a list of the qualities you have chosen to keep for yourself. Use this list as a template for working on and developing these desirable traits until they become your own.

Everyone's childhood is a mixture of good and bad experiences, and every family also has members who are great and some who are difficult. With this exercise, you create a visual experience of the choices you have. As children, we unconsciously learn to emulate the adults around us, but, as adults, we can choose whether we want to adopt every trait or choose some and leave others behind.

The Child You Once Were

Because the child self-underlies your grown-up life, the things you learned in early life are still operating today. Using your self-awareness and self-acceptance to access your child mind allows you to understand the beliefs, experiences, and unresolved problems that can run (and wreak havoc in) your life. This exercise will help you recapture what it was like to be a small child.

EXERCISE

Reclaiming Yourself

1. Your child self. Imagine yourself as a child of 5. Picture yourself as that child surrounded by your early family. Did you have brothers and sisters? How many people were in your home? Where did you live? Picture what your home was like. What colors were the walls? Where did you sleep? Try to get the picture as clear as you can.

2. Getting ready for school. Now, go through a typical school day, beginning with waking up. How do you wake up? How does your morning go? Does someone help you get dressed? Who picks out your clothes? What do you have for breakfast? How do you get to school? What happens on the way?

3. Your day at school. Imagine your school day. Who is your teacher? What do you learn? Who are the other children? What do you have for lunch? Who do you like, and who don't you like? What is the trip home like?

4. After school. What happens when you get home after school? Do you do any homework? Do you go out to play? Who are your playmates? Do you have to do any chores? What happens at dinnertime? What do you eat for supper? Who else is there? What do you do between supper and bedtime? What time do you go to bed?

5. **Questions.** After mentally going through this day, consider the following:

> ➢ What was your role in the family?

> ➢ What role did you play with your friends?

> ➢ Which family members did you have the most contact with?

> ➢ Who was most important to you?

> ➢ Who did you like most?

> ➢ Who did you like least?

> ➢ Who did you try to be like?

> ➢ What would you like to tell yourself as a child?

6. Review. Review the day again, and consider how the ordinary events of normal days influenced who you are. What do you like and not like about how your school and family life influenced you? How can you reject the influences you don't like and enhance the influences you like?

All the experiences, people, habits, rituals, and events of your childhood have a part in shaping who you are today. By looking back at your childhood, you have an opportunity to look with your adult's eyes, understanding, and experience at what life was like for you as a child. Although some of the memories may be painful, this review is valuable because it gives you an opportunity to reevaluate your childhood and understand how it influences you today. When you understand that, you can choose which of your childhood influences you wish to retain and which you want to reject. In this way, you can acquire the power to re-create yourself rather than remain created by your past.

Self-awareness and self-acceptance are basic tools you will use throughout this book and the rest of your life. Your early experience and your observations of others are the raw materials you used to build your worldview and your own attitudes, habits, and beliefs. Next, we'll see how these early childhood experiences shape our adult lives.

Chapter 3. Grown-Up Problems from Family Patterns

The Child is father of the Man.

—William Wordsworth

Does this sound familiar? "I'll never say that to my kids when I grow up!" Most of us said that to ourselves, our friends, or our siblings numerous times throughout childhood. Yet, how often do you find yourself doing or saying things that remind you of your parents or other family members?

Families have sayings; People in my mother's family often said, "The good Lord willin' and the creek don't rise." Members of my Jewish friend's family said, "With one tuchus (butt) you can't dance at two weddings" and "From your mouth to God's ear." My Italian grandfather said, "Di pasta simile son tutti quanti" (They're all made of the same dough). My Texas friend's family said sandpapery things were "rougher than a cob." Families have ritual greetings at holidays, toasts for special occasions, silly sayings that are repeated year after year.

Learning from Family

Sometimes we learn wonderful things from the people we grow up with:

> ➢ Traditional foods, such as the special bread my aunt made for Easter, with whole eggs baked into the crust; or your favorite macaroni and cheese or meatloaf dinner handmade by Mom.

> ➢ Special rituals, such as the story and tuck-in at bedtime, holiday gatherings with the same photo taken of everyone each year, religious observances, or vacation camping trips and summer visits to grandparents.

> ➢ Stories of family history, old songs and poems, games, and values that are passed on from generation to generation.

> ➢ Loving gestures, affectionate memories, precious mementos, and memorable words passed between yourself and other members of your family.

Within our families we learn how to walk, talk, dress, structure time, eat, take care of our hygiene, and relate to each other. All of this is learned before we are old enough to evaluate whether what we are learning is good or bad. Much of what we learn we never think about at all; we just observe what the people around us are doing and imitate it. When we are small, we usually do what we are told without question. Even when small children rebel, they usually don't question what they're rebelling against. They just refuse to do it.

We also learn beliefs and attitudes. Whatever religious information, personal prejudices, educational information, and belief systems our families hold, we learn as unconsciously as we learn to walk and to speak.

Peers also teach us: Neighborhood children, our siblings and cousins, and schoolmates teach us many attitudes and childhood rituals. Games (tag, hide and seek), rhymes (liar, liar, pants on fire), superstitions (step on a crack and break your mother's back,) musical and clothing trends are constantly changing, and, as we get older, they create a wider social sphere.

Learning in Dysfunctional Families

Almost every family provides a mix of good things and dysfunctional behavior. If your genogram exercise from Chapter 1 showed that members of your family exhibited dysfunctional behaviors, those attitudes and beliefs are embedded in your patterns, too.

From exposure to dysfunctional behaviors, you can learn a variety of faulty ideas:

> ➢ It's "normal" to argue, yell, or even be physically violent. This leads to believing that love and anger or violence go hand in hand.

> ➢ Problems aren't solved by discussion. Instead, people either pout silently, talk behind each other's backs, or argue endlessly about who's right and who's wrong.

➤ When someone's feelings are hurt, rather than offer an apology, you get defensive and deny that you did anything hurtful.

➤ When something goes wrong, it's never fixed or forgotten. Grudges are held forever.

➤ Feelings are either overblown and overdramatic or repressed and withheld.

➤ Affection is shown more through teasing and poking fun at each other than genuine expressions of admiration and caring.

➤ Relationships are unfair: Sympathy and favoritism are lavished on one person, blame and criticism on another. Family members "gang up" on each other.

➤ Problems and stress are often dealt with by getting drunk, overspending, overeating, or taking drugs (prescribed or illegal).

These patterns seem "normal" to the children who grow up around them. Because they have little else with which to compare them, children often become adults who find themselves relating in these same dysfunctional ways. For example, Celeste, who was designated the "bad girl" in the family, grows up to have a daughter she describes as a "bad girl." Or Justin, who was taught to be "tough" and not feel his feelings, grows up unable to be affectionate with his family.

As children, we absorb everything that happens around us, and what we experience shapes our beliefs as well as our behavior. Children also are the centers of their own universe, because they don't know enough of life to see life from the viewpoint of others. A child believes she is responsible for everything she experiences. She sees a direct cause and effect relationship. For example, if a parent is irritable, cold, or upset, the child feels somehow responsible.

When Dad comes home from work tired and irritable from a bad drive and doesn't greet 2-year-old Sally with his usual hug and happy greeting, Sally is upset and frightened, believing it is somehow her fault. If this cold, angry behavior happens only once in a while, Sally will quickly get over it and learn over time how to handle such moods. But if Dad is habitually angry and cold, Sally will grow up expecting that all men are like that and will perhaps act in defensive and suspicious ways that encourage some men to treat her badly. Because of her childhood-based belief, she will find this treatment "normal" and accept it. The bad treatment from men will then reinforce her belief that men are cold and angry and that she is unlovable and worthless.

When, as children, we are loved and supported, the problems we face become learning opportunities and we eventually learn to handle problems, disappointments, and failure with a positive attitude. On the other hand, if we are seldom encouraged, taught, or interacted with, we deal with the stress and emotional pain of rejection and alienation by developing beliefs that "explain" why life is so difficult.

If Mother is sometimes sad or goes through a difficult life experience, such as the death of a relative, her son Johnny can learn to be sympathetic and also acquire some tools for grieving in his own life. But if Mother is clinically depressed and sad most of the time, Johnny learns that having fun is wrong, that misery is acceptable, and, because he gets little interaction with his mom, he may wind up feeling responsible for his mother's sadness and feel hopeless and helpless about life. As an adult, he may be attracted to depressed and helpless women and feel joyless and responsible for everything. Johnny may grow up to be the type of man who dies early of a heart attack, which is a research-proven result of stress, loneliness, and misery.

According to Proverbs, "As the twig is bent, so grows the tree." These famous words reflect the truth that, unless something is done to recognize and change the patterns, childhood influences create belief systems and behaviors that persist throughout life as an adult.

Family Patterns Checklist

This checklist will help you to discover your family patterns. The options listed for each situation are suggestions. Feel free to supply your own answers, if they differ from the common reactions shown here. Different family members may have different reactions, and you may want to consider different family members (for example, if your grandparents were a big part of childhood, or if an older sibling did a lot of parenting of you, or if you yourself were in the parent position as a child) than the ones I mention in the examples.

1. When my parents disagreed, they:
   a. Fought
   b. Were silent
   c. Got drunk
   d. Had hysterics
   e. Tried to get the kids to take sides
   f. Worked it out

2. When events were stressful, my parents:
   a. Yelled and fought
   b. Were reassuring and supportive
   c. Pretended nothing was wrong
   d. Called a family conference to discuss the problem
   e. Panicked, made bad decisions
   f. Got depressed or even drunk

3. Holidays were usually:
   a. Upsetting
   b. Boring
   c. Warm and loving
   d. Full of tradition and ritual
   e. Ignored
   f. Occasions for overindulging in food and/or drink

4. Money was handled:
   a. Competently, with an eye toward the future
   b. Lavishly, with overspending and extravagance
   c. Nervously, with a lot of worry and confusion

    d.   Tightly, with stinginess and fear

    e.   Scarcely, with poverty, not much was available

    f.   Irresponsibly, wasted on drugs, gambling, or other addictions

5.   The family attitude toward school was:

    a.   It's important, do your homework, get good marks, we'll help you if you need it

    b.   It's your problem, don't bother me about it

    c.   You'll be punished if you don't do well

    d.   Being popular is more important than being smart

    e.   If you don't do well, you won't get into college, you'll be a failure at life

    f.   Book learning is not important; blue collar work is what counts

6.   Mealtimes were:

    a.   Rushed and haphazard

    b.   Nonexistent—everyone ate separately

    c.   Stiff and formal

    d.   Family times for great conversation and home- cooked food

    e.   Mostly takeout, but fun

    f.   Eaten in front of the TV

7.   Bedtimes were:

    a.   Whenever we wanted

    b.   Strictly enforced

    c.   Cozy and relaxed, with a story and a tuck-in

    d.   Stressful, everyone got cranky

    e.   Quiet and restful

    f.   Noisy

8. The family attitude toward religion was:

   a. Casual: church occasionally, especially Easter and Christmas

   b. Devout: church school, weekly services or masses, communion, bar mitzvah, prayers at home

   c. Atheist: existence of God denied, or no religious talk allowed

   d. Agnostic: lots of philosophical argument and discussion, no religious observance

   e. Not manly: women and children observed religion, men did not

   f. Confusing: parents were from different religions

9. Relatives were:

   a. Rarely around, lived far away

   b. Around for every holiday

   c. Numerous and always there

   d. Boring: old, distant

   e. Fun: lots of young cousins, played games and sports

   f. Scary: fought a lot or drank too much

10. If you were ill:

    a. You got a lot of care and attention

    b. You stayed home from school

    c. You were ignored

    d. You weren't believed

    e. You saw a doctor

    f. You were treated with home remedies, chicken soup, and so on

After you've considered all the questions, compare the answers about your family to your life now. What attitudes and behaviors have you changed since you grew up? What has remained the same? How do your current relationships resemble your family? Do you still treat money, holidays, meals, illness, religion, and people in similar ways?

Seek to achieve an objective evaluation of what you experienced in childhood and how those experiences influenced your current choices, behaviors, and beliefs.

Beliefs, Attitudes, and Behavior

As children, we first learn behavior in the family setting, then later, as we try to make sense of things, we form beliefs around those behaviors. For example, if being sick meant getting a lot of attention, which was hard to come by normally, you may find you tend to get colds when you are having a difficult time in life and need some reassurance.

Let's examine some examples of beliefs people grow up with as a result of family experience.

Money

Objectively viewed, money is a simple tool that allows you to transform your work into an easily portable way to buy what you want. But in real life, money is a symbol for many different things. It can be a substitute for or expression of love, power, self-worth, social status, security, intelligence, fear, or ethics. For example:

➢ **Scarcity:** Adults whose childhood was spent in difficult, poverty-ridden circumstances, or a war situation where money and food were scarce, or some other experience of want, often grow up with a consciousness of scarcity and an imbalance with money. Either they continue to live in poverty or, if they have learned how to make money, they can have problems with overspending or being too miserly.

➢ **Love or approval:** If money was used to show love or approval in childhood the adult can grow up to give overly lavish presents, and to buy love and friendship, or only to value others who have a lot of money.

➤ **Power:** If money was used as the determining factor of who got their way—for example, a working father with a non-working wife who always deferred to him—kids might grow up to feel that the amount of money one has determines their position in life. The recent stories of top executives who cheat and steal funds are illustrations of people who would do anything for more money and who view money as necessary for personal power.

➤ **Social status:** For children who grew up in poverty or in a minority group, money often becomes a symbol for social acceptability. These adults often are focused on fashionable, expensive brand names, and status symbols, such as extravagant cars and palatial homes. Sometimes, the need for these prestigious possessions leads to massive debt.

➤ **Security/comfort:** Oftentimes, money is used as a way to make a child feel better: "Poor baby, your friend hurt your feelings? Let's go buy you a new toy and you'll feel better." An adult can grow up to use money as a way to avoid feelings of fear, hurt, anger, or grief. Money used this way becomes a spending or gambling addiction.

➤ **Functional:** A family with a healthy attitude toward money models how to save it and when and how to spend it appropriately and wisely, and uses it as the tool it really is. Adults who were raised with this attitude feel comfortable with their money.

These are just some examples of the various attitudes families can have about money and some of the possible results. When you consider your own family's finances, look at the patterns that were provided, and see how they have affected you.

Health

Our bodies require cleanliness, nutrition, exercise, and sometimes medical attention to stay healthy. Stress, a poor diet, lack of hygiene, exposure to disease, accidental injury, and genetic conditions can all contribute to serious and debilitating health problems. But even the minor, common childhood health problems, such as colds and upset tummies, will produce family reactions that can influence a child's beliefs:

➢ **Anxiety:** When every little ailment is greeted with an overanxious response, children can grow into adults who are hypochondriacal, obsess over their health, and visit the doctor for every little symptom.

➢ **Indulgence:** If Mom makes special foods, lets you stay home from school, and fusses over you the entire time you're sick, you might grow up to be an adult who gets sick whenever you feel the need for comfort.

➢ **Stress:** A highly stressed family is often also a family whose members are frequently sick. Illness increases the stress, and increased stress exacerbates illness, so it becomes a vicious cycle. Under this kind of stress, very often the sickest person is the one who gets the most attention. This combination of stress and reward can lead to or worsen chronic illnesses, such as irritable bowel syndrome, asthma, and acid reflux disease.

➢ **Balance:** Emotionally healthy families approach the issue of staying physically and emotionally healthy in a balanced fashion. Such families focus on a healthy diet, exercise, emotional stability, and relaxed living. They also focus on disease prevention with regular medical checkups. Children who grow up in this atmosphere learn the needed tools and options for maintaining their optimum health without undue effort.

How did your family's health focus compare to these examples? Are you still viewing your health in the same way?

Food

Nutrition seems pretty basic: three square meals a day, not too many sweets, moderation of the junk, and you're okay. In practice in your family, however, it may have been a lot more confusing. Even the government has revised a lot of its guidelines in the new food pyramid. Conflicting and bewildering theories and recommendations abound in the media. Families may try to sort their way through this maze, or just follow tradition—but whose tradition? Kosher, Italian, Japanese, Korean, Vietnamese, Chinese, Thai, Indian, Soul, Southwestern, Cajun, Tex-Mex, American, Mexican, you name it. We all enjoy all these cuisines to varying degrees. Families who come from these backgrounds have other traditions and emotions that are connected to the food. Nutritionists know that certain diseases are more prevalent in certain ethnic communities who stick to their traditional diet, whereas other cultures have diets that are healthier. Recently, the Mediterranean diet and the Japanese diet earned a lot of media attention for being healthy, and other cuisines, such as Southern, Cajun, and French, have been criticized for being unhealthy, leading to weight problems, diabetes, and heart disease.

Here are some examples of how families might approach food:

➤ **Ethnic:** Families who cook a traditional ethnic cuisine often have religious and cultural meaning tied up in every bite. It really feels as if you are what you eat. But, in many cases, the cultural cuisine brings a lot of problems with it. Although it has a lot of emotional (and often religious) significance, ethnic food can be too fatty, unbalanced, or overcooked or contain too many sweets for good health. To change your diet from the way your mom cooked can feel like betrayal of your family history and tradition.

➤ **Indulgent:** If your mom's greatest joy was to bake or buy treats for you, or your dad was a gourmet cook or loved to barbecue ribs, or every holiday and gathering was all about eating all you could hold, or your family celebrated special occasions in fine restaurants, then food takes on a special significance, and becomes permanently entangled with love. From the earliest moments, an infant experiences at the breast that love and food are inextricably tied. Food is naturally symbolic of comfort and well-being, and, when this connection is emphasized and exaggerated, it can easily lead to lifelong problems of overindulgence.

➤ **Haphazard:** Some families are disjointed and haphazard, and mealtimes are irregular, at best. Often, such families eat on the run and seldom sit down together. Sometimes, everyone except the smallest children is on his or her own to figure out what and when to eat. Food is often snack food or fast food, and the closest they get to home-cooked food is a frozen dinner or take-out. With such a history, children can grow up with poor eating habits and nutrition.

As adults, they can be uncomfortable in normal eating situations, such as at fine restaurants or a formal dinner at someone's home. The thought of cooking dinner, of course, would be a mystery. Sometimes, a child who grows up in such a home will become focused on food in an attempt to replace what's missing. Ironically, this child may become a gourmet cook or professional chef.

➤ **Pressure:** Families that are very regulated may put heavy pressure on children to eat certain ways, have extremely correct manners, or eat foods they don't like. Other families may argue or fight at the dinner table. This kind of pressure can cause children to grow up with eating disorders, such as anorexia, or to be extremely picky about food. It takes the joy out of eating and replaces it with tension.

➤ **Anxiety/deprivation: In** highly anxious families, mealtimes just add to the stress. Perhaps money and food are scarce, or the family style may simply be to worry about everything during dinner, which creates a tense atmosphere. Children who grow up in such tension may become adults with anxiety-related digestive problems, such as irritable bowel syndrome, gall bladder problems, or acid reflux. They may not feel comfortable in social situations that involve meals or in any situation that is reminiscent of childhood meals.

➤ **Balance:** Balanced families focus on good nutrition and can still indulge in occasional desserts and have fun with food. If their cultural roots include food that is unhealthy, they learn how to eat it in moderation at ceremonial times, and eat healthier foods or healthy modifications of their traditional meals most of the time. Healthy families can accept the individual likes and dislikes of various members. They recognize that food can be a source of comfort, but they seek to enjoy food in moderation. Healthy families frequently sit down to meals together. Mealtimes are relaxed and organized, times of sharing and enjoying each other, as well as the food. Children are taught good table manners but not made anxious about the issue. As they grow up, both boys and girls are taught age-appropriate cooking skills, so by the time they are grown, they are self-sufficient about food and cooking and are comfortable dining out.

Time

There are a limited number of hours in every day, and how families make use of time affects many other things in life. Although the average family has much more "leisure time" (nonworking hours) than the working family of 100 years ago, the modern family seems to try to cram more and more activities into every week. Many modern conveniences allow us to do things much more quickly but also seem to wind up absorbing time. For example, with the car and modern roads, we can travel so much faster and farther than families early in the last century, and as a result we seem to be on the go all the time. The computer enables us to communicate all over the world at the blink of a modem, but it also winds up being a "time sink" that absorbs endless hours before we know it. Television brings entertainment into our living rooms and also uses up hours per week. Time is also symbolic, and time spent with family is interpreted as an expression of love. We are all familiar with the expression "time is money." Often, the pursuit of money (even just enough to live on comfortably) makes it difficult for families to find enough time together. The large number of single-parent and divorced families also find time scarce in their situations.

> **Feeling rushed:** In some families, there never seems to be enough time to go around. Meals are rushed, homework and housework are slap-dash, and the family rarely gets time to just hang out together. Families in this situation often waste large amounts of time watching TV, or parents spend long hours at work and have too little time at home. Sometimes the family is overscheduled, with organized clubs, classes, and sports taking up all their free time. Children who grow up in this situation often become adults who are stressed about time and rarely feel that they have time to relax. When they do get some free time, they often feel fidgety and lost, not knowing how to enjoy it. Of course, all of these time pressures can add to stress and anxiety.

> **Procrastination:** Families who procrastinate never get around to finishing what they start or perhaps never get started in the first place. They are generally habitually late. The attitude in these families is: "I'll think about that tomorrow." These are people who wait until the last minute to pack for vacation, or to begin a school science project, and often stay up late at night to meet some deadline. Curiously, procrastination is often closely tied to perfectionism. Perfectionists often stall on doing projects because

they haven't gotten everything perfectly prepared. Adults who grew up in a procrastinating family often have trouble getting anywhere on time, even to work. They sometimes work well under pressure but don't get anything done until the last minute. Other times, they become paralyzed by the pressure of time, and sometimes even depressed.

➤ **Regimented:** Time can rule in certain families. Bedtime, waking time, meals, and every other event are timed to the minute. Being ready on time is expected; being late is a major error. Military families sometimes have this attitude toward time. Children raised this way grow up to be rigid about schedules and get very upset if normal delays occur. They are slaves to the clock.

➤ **Scarce:** Some families approach time as if there will never be enough. "Hurry up" is the watchword. Often, single parents treat time this way, because a single parent has more to do in the same amount of time. Two-career parents can also be rushed. Children feel rushed and anxious, and they may never get the necessary time to dawdle and play creatively. They often grow up to be tense and hurried adults, who find it impossible to sit still for long.

➤ **Shared:** Families who see time as something to share with each other, and who manage it calmly and with balance, seek to enjoy whatever time they have together. Rather than focusing on how little free time they have, filling up every minute with scheduled activities, or living every moment by the clock, they divide their days up reasonably, allowing time for relaxation, time for work and homework, time for household chores and meals, and time for fun. Adults raised in such families are not anxious or stressed about their schedules and know how to use time as a tool and a resource. They make the most of their available time and use it wisely.

Disagreements

No couple or family gets through life without conflict. It's normal for people to disagree and even to be out of sorts from time to time. How such clashes are handled is the key to whether they turn into fights or productive negotiations. What happens in the family determines what children learn about working through differences and solving problems.

➤ **Fights:** When families don't have negotiation skills and respect for one another, disagreements quickly become fights. Fights between parents frighten and upset children and teach them that fighting is the way to deal with problems. Children in this situation learn very little impulse control and no skills for negotiating and calming tense situations. As adults, they feel helpless in the face of disagreements and are liable to be very reactive. They have not learned to think constructively about what they're trying to accomplish. If the fights and arguments in the early family are violent, the child learns that someone has to be the perpetrator and someone has to be the victim. When children become adults, they can wind up in either or both of these roles, but they will still feel totally out of control. Fighting in families is often exacerbated by drugs and alcohol. This sets up a vicious cycle, where the fighting creates hurt feelings and tension, both of which are self-medicated with drugs or alcohol. The substance abuse relaxes inhibitions, which makes fighting and violence more likely and more dramatic.

➤ **Power plays:** In some families, winning is the most important thing. Arguments are about who is right, who wins, who gets his or her way. This is very dysfunctional, because a lot of energy is wasted on endless struggle that solves nothing. Children in this family learn hopelessness and hyper-vigilance—at the drop of a hat, their parents can erupt in a yelling match that seems endless and that solves nothing. As adults, these children are abrasive, irritable, and easily set off. They tend to be controlling, trying to keep life within bounds.

➤ **Silence:** Some families are so worried about disagreements, and feel so incapable of resolving them; they try to avoid the whole problem by ignoring it. This leads to distance, coldness, and resulting resentment. Once problems or disagreements occur, they stay around forever. There is no hope of solving them because no one can talk about them. Children learn not to express their wants and feelings, because if they say the "wrong thing," the silence will descend and isolate them. These children can grow up to be repressed and depressed adults.

➤ **Taking sides:** Other families handle disagreements as political campaigns or lawsuits. Rather than dealing directly with each other, each person tries to enlist others on his or her side. Families become a hotbed of intrigue, with everyone manipulating each other and talking behind backs. They work on the "persecutor—rescuer—victim" model, where someone is always the "poor victim" and someone else is the "bad guy" and a third person is making things worse by "trying to help." The family can be likened to a soap opera, full of unnecessary drama and stress. Children in such families learn to manipulate, be indirect, and sneak around. The patterns learned here can create an adult life full of drama and stress. Adults from these families can duplicate the interactions with friends, at work and in their personal relationships.

➢ **Discussions:** If disagreements lead to discussions that solve problems, the relationship and the family are strengthened each time. Everyone involved learns more skills and finds new options for whatever problems arise. After a few years of successful problem-solving in this manner, everyone in the family becomes expert at smoothly handling differences and coming up with mutually satisfactory solutions. Children who grow up in this environment learn many communication and coping skills, which are modeled in the family. They grow up to be adults who can manage people with a high degree of success, who have many satisfying friendships, and who are capable of creating dynamic, effective, and gratifying partnerships.

Stress

Stress is also a part of everyday life for all families. There's the normal stress of earning a living, managing money and time, handling children and schoolwork, and all the other aspects of daily living. On top of the normal stressors, there are the extra-stressful events, such as illness, accidents, loss of jobs, major car or home repairs, and other unforeseen circumstances. Every family encounters such problems, and how they handle them can determine how the children who grow up in the family will handle stress many years later.

➢ **Blaming:** Families who spend time pointing fingers at each other with an "it's all your fault" attitude just increase the stress and resentment involved. The more the blaming and defending escalate, the harder it is for family members to think clearly and make good decisions about the stressful situation. Responding without clear thinking can make problems worse, so the situation continues to escalate and the stress gets worse and worse. Children who grow up in this environment often have stress-related health problems, such as asthma; anxiety attacks; and sleep; eating, or digestive disorders. They can also become adults who are over- reactive to stress, and become easily overwhelmed or upset.

➢ **Avoiding:** In some families, dealing with stressful issues, such as financial or health problems, is avoided. The family just ignores the problem, until it grows so huge it cannot be ignored any longer. This has a similar effect to the blaming response, in that it increases rather than handles problems as well as the related stress. Children in this atmosphere also have stress-related symptoms and learn to avoid dealing directly with problems. They may grow up to feel paralyzed in the face of stressful events they should normally be able to handle.

➢ **Shifting responsibility:** Some families try to get someone else to take responsibility for a problem. These families try to shift the burden of handling the stress to someone else, or they try to pawn it off on each other. "You help the children with homework; I'm too busy." Or they try to transfer the problem to someone outside the family, such as by yelling at the teacher or the school board. This process wastes a lot of energy that could be used better in actually solving the problem. Instead, it keeps everyone busy and allows them to feel that they're doing something about it, without having to come up with a real solution. Children in these families grow up trying to avoid being pinpointed as the responsible party. They may hide out in times of stress and learn to keep a low profile, or to maneuver other members. They don't know who to trust. Older children learn to manipulate more naive younger siblings, and younger siblings learn to collapse into tears, to get someone to step in on their behalf. As adults, these children become prime movers of office intrigue who cannot trust or be trusted.

➢ **Facing the problem:** Families who have the necessary skill and awareness to work together to reduce stress and solve problems fare better than the previous examples. In these more functional families, everyone is more relaxed, and life feels a lot more sensible and manageable. Hence, stress is reduced. Knowing other family members will work with you to help you solve problems is comforting and reassuring and indicates a level of mutual trust and accountability. Children in such families learn to work with others to create a mutually helpful atmosphere and reduce the stress on everyone. They grow up to be adults who work well with others, whose lives seem to be blessed, because they don't add to the unavoidable stresses life presents.

Illness

Illness comes in many varieties in families, from a child's upset tummy through the usual childhood colds, chicken pox, and measles, to serious and chronic ailments, problems requiring surgery, or even terminal illnesses. Every family has a style for handling illness, from which children can form habits and belief systems.

> ➤ **Pampering:** If a minor childhood illness means that Mom makes special foods, lets you stay home from school, plays games with you, and generally treats you better than any other time, you may learn that being slightly ill is a great way to get attention without really being in severe ill health. Adults who grew up with this attitude toward illness may tend to be caregivers, but also have minor illnesses in times of stress. For example, such an adult may get a cold or a headache when facing a big business presentation or a college exam.

> ➤ **Hypochondria:** In some families, every illness, no matter how small, is a major cause of hysteria. The whole family panics and is mobilized. If the medical doctor says the ailment is not much of a problem, the family gets angry, rather than relieved, at the doctor. Children learn that illness is dramatic, important, and mysterious, and they crave the attention it brings, while simultaneously fearing it. As adults, they may be obsessively worried about their health, illness, and disease.

> ➤ **Isolation:** Some families treat their members who are ill as pariahs, leaving them alone, giving them "space"—but, also, often neglecting them. This may be because of a belief that healing is best done alone, or it may be out of not knowing what to do, or it may be out of an aversion to being around someone who is ill. Children learn to be very self-sufficient in illness and grow up to be adults who do not want tender ministrations when they are not feeling well.

> **Folk and family remedies:** Tradition is very strong in some families, especially those with a deep connection to ethnic roots. In times when access to medicine and medical knowledge was rare, people relied on herbal remedies and folklore to heal illness. Some of these remedies were (and remain) very effective (for example, aspirin was originally derived from willow bark, which many cultures used as a tea for pain) while others were bogus. Still, healing lore is very helpful in many families, and there often is a grandmother or aunt who always seems to have something that will help a small problem or ease it until the doctor is consulted. These family remedies are beneficial unless they are connected with a belief system that prevents the family from seeking medical care when it is needed. Children from these families often learn healing lore from their elders, and can grow up to be very good at caretaking, which is a great asset, unless it is distorted by problematic beliefs.

> **Balanced:** Families who are calm and rational about illness will assess the problem, and sometimes apply natural remedies, such as cold packs for bruises or mint tea for minor digestive problems. They also consult a doctor if the problem is serious or they cannot fix it easily. They focus on preventive care, making sure children get enough sleep, proper nutrition, and exercise, and they create a calm, caring environment that is conducive to health. Children who grow up in such families understand that nutrition, sleep, and exercise all contribute to good health and grow into adults who have the confidence they'll know what to do in the event of illness.

Sleep

According to Shakespeare's Lady Macbeth, an original dysfunctional family member, it is sleep "that knitteth up the raveled sleeve of care." Sleep is essential to physical health and mental well-being. But from the newborn's need for food and changing every two hours in the first weeks of life, sleep issues can easily become a problem. How families handle sleep and bedtime is yet another way the children are shaped into adults.

> **Unregulated:** Some families seem to pay little attention to sleep. Children are allowed to stay up as late as they want and are not given curfews or regular bedtimes. One sibling in such a family may be an early-to-bed, early-to- rise child and another may turn out to

be a "night owl." Children growing up under these conditions may find a rhythm that works for them, and others may not ever learn how to create regular sleeping hours. When grown, children who have not learned a regular bedtime might have trouble adjusting to the requirements of getting up for work and may habitually not get enough sleep or suffer from insomnia.

➤ **Regimented:** In the regimented family, sleep, like time, is handled on a strict schedule. Bedtimes are enforced, and there is no adjustment for special circumstances. Children learn to sleep on demand and find it hard to deal with changes in schedules when they grow up.

➤ **Emotional:** Whether people sleep in some families depends on the emotional climate. Sleep ranges from sleeping all day when people feel down, to not sleeping at all when they're excited or anxious. Children learn erratic sleep habits and grow up not knowing how to regulate their sleeping by calming themselves down.

➤ **Balanced:** Healthy families know that sufficient sleep is important and make sure the evening calms down a while before a bedtime that is early enough to ensure enough sleep. Bedtime includes preparation rituals such as brushing teeth, bedtime stories, and prayers, all of which help calm the children down and provide a natural progression toward sleep. Children in this family learn a healthy respect for sleep, without being rigid. When the day has been exciting, they know how to calm themselves down and prepare for bedtime. As adults, they have little trouble getting sufficient sleep or creating the proper atmosphere for falling asleep.

Religion

At one time, it was fairly unusual for families to have to deal with differences in religion. When the society was less mobile, most people stayed where they were, in homogenous groups, and married close to home. Religious options were few, especially in smaller towns. Jews and Christians did not mix much, and ethnic groups stayed separate, keeping their religions separate also. Religious traditions were passed down with related food, rituals, holidays, and value systems. Today, all those taboos have been breached. Families today are made up of all kinds of ethnic and religious mixes. Our polyglot society is reflected within the family. In this mixed atmosphere, religion can become a source of contention. How a family handles things unseen has a great deal of influence on the values of everyone involved.

➢ **Avoidance:** Couples who never spoke of spiritual matters before getting married can wind up with huge conflicts, especially when one partner is from a strict religious background with which the other is uncomfortable. Often, the couple can accommodate their differences until they have children, and then the issue of how the children will be raised becomes intense. Rather than argue, some families solve this problem by deciding to ignore it. No one talks about religion at all, and the children have no spiritual orientation. As adults, they don't know what they believe and often go on a search for meaning.

➢ **Devout:** Some families have a clear spiritual or religious orientation and keep strict observances. This may be done in a joyous, fulfilling way or be joyless and oppressive. Children can be given a strong foundation or feel trapped in a series of rules that don't feel good. If the child happens to be different than the religion's tenets allow, it can set up an identity crisis. For example, a child who is gay and grows up in an antigay religious household, or a female child who grows up in a religion that oppresses women, can feel worthless and unacceptable because of the conflict between the religious beliefs and their own identity.

➢ **Confused/conflicted:** When family members (especially the parents) have different beliefs, and they struggle or argue rather than finding a mutually acceptable solution, they create both confusion and conflict within the members. Children in such families have a problem knowing what to believe. Sometimes different children side with different parents, or one child will be left with conflicting beliefs. Adults who were raised in such a situation either grow up searching to define their own beliefs (which can be painful but helpful) or ignoring the entire question, and feeling confused and unresolved. This may not be a problem until a crisis arises or until the person develops a serious relationship with someone who has clear religious views.

> **Competitive:** When the differing religions turn competitive, and the extended families (for example, one Jewish, one Catholic) get into the struggle, with each side arguing about how the children will be raised and about which religion is better, everyone suffers. The children are caught between two systems of belief and have no way of resolving the issue. This can be extremely painful for children who feel torn because they love their parents and other relatives. It can produce an adult who is agnostic, believing religion is just a source of emotional pain and conflict.

> **Open-minded:** Families who have the values that a balanced religion can provide and are willing to discuss questions and consider differences give their children a solid grounding from which they can later make their own decisions. Parents who are from different religions, but who discuss and work out how they'll handle the differences in an amiable manner, preferably before they have children, can present a balanced viewpoint for their children and even help them understand that they come from more than one culture and viewpoint. In such a case, parents can make sure that other relatives understand and respect their decision, so the children aren't pulled in different directions by other family members. Their children can grow up to be reasonable and rational about religious matters and tolerant of the beliefs of others.

Holidays

Religious holidays, work holidays, vacations, parties, birthdays, anniversaries, and other special events can be times of celebration or times of stress and drama. How a family approaches and carries out celebrations and anniversaries often defines their style of having fun, and their group dynamic.

> **Extravagant:** Some families go all out on the holidays, with lavish meals, expensive presents, and spectacular rituals or intricate traditions. It is not only desired, but expected, that all family members will be present for every major holiday. This creates pressure, financially and otherwise. For example, a family member who wants to diet is pressured to eat the rich food, or another who has lost a job feels obligated to buy expensive gifts. Also, the ritual and extravagance can mask an emptiness of meaning or feeling.

Sometimes people who have trouble with intimacy try to make up for it with money. Children who grow up in this atmosphere can become adults who overdo everything. They overwhelm their friends with lavish, inappropriate gifts, and they have conflict in relationships when a partner wants to be with his or her own family for the holidays.

➤ **Practical:** Families with a practical approach to the holidays can deal with changes and realities but often miss out on the magic. They may decide that the holiday is too much trouble, or not want to spend any money, and therefore miss out on the fun. They may do such practical things on holidays that it's difficult to discern what is special about the day. Children who grow up this way may have trouble figuring out how to celebrate effectively.

➤ **Perfectionistic:** In some families, holiday celebrations have to be "just so." They are not necessarily lavish or expensive, but they can be fussy. Family members can wind up fretting more about how things are done than enjoying each other. The meaning of the holiday can be eclipsed by the minutia of the details. Children who grow up this way become focused on the particulars of special occasions, and as adults they can have trouble relaxing and enjoying holidays with others who do it differently.

➤ **Tension-filled:** When families don't get along, their holiday celebrations can become tense and unpleasant, with frequent arguments, backbiting, and gossip. Family members can avoid attending because the experience is not enjoyable. Children who grow up in this atmosphere do not feel good about holidays and grow into adults who avoid such occasions, perhaps staying home alone, or going skiing over Christmas, or traveling to other countries on holidays.

➤ **Convivial:** Holidays for some families are wonderful occasions to be together, to have a relaxed and enjoyable time, made special by some traditional foods and rituals, but not obsessed with them. The point is clearly for everyone to have a good time, to commemorate the occasion, to build and share memories, and to reaffirm their family history and connection. New people are welcomed into these occasions. The family may miss an absent member but does not consider it a betrayal for someone to be somewhere else. Children in these families have fond memories of holidays past, enjoy the current holidays, and as adults are capable of creating warm occasions on their own, when necessary. These adults are the people everyone wants to be around on special occasions.

Education

Some families value formal education, some pass wisdom down from older generations, and some don't seem to value knowledge much at all. Yet, the level of education a person achieves often determines income, status, and the quality of his or her life. So, how your family teaches you to feel about education as a child can have a profound impact on your life as an adult.

➤ **Pressure:** When getting an education becomes more important than being happy or successful, the family has become obsessed with the idea of education and has lost sight of the real reasons for acquiring knowledge. For these families, education might seem to be the only route to success, and they may pressure children to get better marks, to do excessive amounts of studying, and to succeed at all costs. They may also put pressure on teachers and school administrators. Of course, education is valuable, but these parents don't recognize there are other viable routes to success and fulfillment. Children in education-obsessed families can feel pressured and resistant to education or helpless and stupid if they don't do well. Children who have other talents, such as art, mechanics, or computers, may not be supported in pursuing careers that would be fulfilling to them. They may grow up to be adults who wind up in careers they don't like or who feel like failures because they didn't succeed academically.

➤ **Ridicule/hostility:** When a family does not value education at all, they may make fun of a smart child, calling him or her a "nerd" and valuing the sports prowess or music talent of other siblings more. The family may feel denigrated because they are not as interested in education as the clever child. Children whose intelligence and bookishness are ridiculed, and who are not encouraged, may still succeed with the support of teachers or others, but the price they pay is high. They may feel alienated from their families, and the family may intensify this by telling such children they "think they're better than" the rest of the family. As adults, these children might succeed scholastically and career-wise but be undermined by low self-esteem and have trouble bonding successfully with others.

> **Indifference:** Some families are too stressed or dysfunctional to care about whether children are good in school or not. They don't pay attention to homework, show up at parent/teacher night, or show interest in their children's scholastic achievements. Children succeed or fail on their own or because of the interest and support of people outside the family. They grow up feeling that they have to do it alone and that educational achievement is a way to be unpopular, if successful. This makes them insecure in friendships and relationships.

> **Support:** Families that support education without pushing it too hard are interested in the children's schoolwork and encourage kids to talk about what is happening and what they are learning. They support science fairs and back-to- school night and are available to help with homework, although they don't overdo it. They meet with teachers and help their children with social as well as academic skills. They also recognize that there are other ways to be smart besides academics. They support and encourage children in expressing whatever talents they have. If a child wants to write poetry, or loves animals, or is artistic or obsessed with making movies or programming or building computers, the family encourages expression of those things, while also making sure the child keeps up schoolwork and social activities. Knowing that children often have temporary obsessions that eventually pass and that a true vocation won't show itself until later, parents stress that a balanced life is important. Children in this family learn that whatever they're interested in is important, and they get well-rounded experience. As adults, they are comfortable expressing themselves in many ways, and in choosing a career they focus on their strengths and what they enjoy doing, which means they have a better chance of choosing a satisfying career and getting whatever kind of education or training they need to be successful.

Cleanliness

No home stays clean on its own. Every family has a style and an attitude about cleanliness. Whose responsibility is cleaning the house? Caring for the outside? Maintaining the car? Taking out the garbage? How are those decisions made? How important is cleanliness, and what is the definition of "clean"? How your family answers these questions will impact your attitudes as an adult.

> **Perfectionist:** Families with impossible standards of cleanliness, where everything has to be neat and organized at all times, can create a tense and stifling atmosphere. Chores are overemphasized and too extreme, and children cannot relax or make a mess. Pets are not allowed because they're dirty. Certain activities are too messy. These children learn to dampen their enthusiasm and feel anxious about making a mistake. As adults, they react to this childhood by either giving up on cleanliness altogether, because they resent the pressure, or they are extra neat. They may have trouble living with people who are not as neat, and messy activities, such as sex, can be problematic.

> **Messy:** In other families, cleanliness is not important at all. The house is usually a mess, and, although kitchen and bathrooms may be clean, clutter is everywhere. There may be piles of dirty (or clean but unfolded) laundry, old newspapers, and other disorganized stuff. Children in this family may be relaxed, but they don't learn any housekeeping skills. When they grow up, they have no idea how to keep a pleasant, tidy home. They may also have problems with housemates who are annoyed by their messy habits.

> **Inequitable:** If household chores are unfairly divided in the family, problems can also result. If Mom does everything and asks no one else (or only the girls) to help, she is teaching gender role attitudes to both her sons and daughters. If certain children (the girls, or the eldest) are given disproportionate responsibility for chores, they will feel resentful and persecuted. These attitudes can remain with children into adulthood.

> **Pleasantly clean:** If cleanliness makes sense and is relatively organized but not rigid, and chores are appropriately and fairly distributed, the household runs smoothly. This requires communication and negotiation ability within the family, and children learn these skills as well as the housekeeping skills they need to be self-sufficient adults. A well- run but not unreasonably strict home is a pleasant place to be. If children learn that helping to keep things orderly and clean is a normal part of belonging in a family, they don't resent chores, and they grow up to be orderly and competent homemakers as adults.

Of course, there are many more styles and attitudes of family life than I have presented here, but hopefully this smattering presents enough examples that you will be able to see glimpses of your own family history and be able to infer how they remain with you to this day.

EXERCISE

Family Styles

In a notebook or journal, list each category discussed in the previous section, as follows:

- ➤ **Money**
- ➤ **Illness**
- ➤ **Health**
- ➤ **Sleep**
- ➤ **Food**
- ➤ **Religion**
- ➤ **Time**
- ➤ **Holidays**
- ➤ **Disagreements**
- ➤ **Education**
- ➤ **Stress**
- ➤ **Cleanliness**

Next to each category, write a brief description of how your own family handled each item. Use your family map from Chapter 1 to help you remember. Keep in mind that a family that is dysfunctional about one area, such as money or cleanliness, can be very healthy in other areas, such as time or food. Knowing how your actions and interactions today are affected by your childhood family will help you to use the exercises and information in the rest of the book more effectively.

Chapter 4: Why Do I Do That? The Child Running the Adult

I do not do the good I want, but the evil I do not want is what I do.
—Paul, to the Romans

Whether or not you're religious, you surely recognize this feeling. Each of us has noble goals and ideals we'd like to achieve, but we often find ourselves acting in exactly opposite ways. It's upsetting and mystifying to realize:

➤ Because you were angry, you said things you didn't mean.

➤ Because you were tired or hurt, you broke your diet.

➤ Because you were distracted, you missed a stop sign while driving.

➤ Because you were upset, you fell off the wagon.

➤ Because you were lonely, you wound up in another abusive relationship.

It's also frustrating and discouraging to:

➤ Make the same mistakes over and over.

➤ Not be able to finish what you start.

➤ Have dreams but never be able to make them real.

➤ Let your friends and family down repeatedly.

➤ Be used by people you care about.

➤ Be too afraid to do what you want.

➤ Not be in control of your spending, drinking, emotions, or relationships.

➤ Generally feel like you're not in charge of your own life.

Out of Control

It's difficult, if not impossible, to get ahead in your life when you can't control your feelings or actions. When it feels as if an enemy lives inside you and takes over the minute your guard is down, you can't trust yourself, no matter how good your intentions and motives are.

> Lydia, a 26-year-old mother, comes to me in tears, confessing that she's endangering her family and her own life with her sexual addiction. Her husband has suspected her many times, but she has managed to convince him she's faithful. However, her dysfunctional family background has caused her to crave the attention and excitement of illicit sex. Although she gave up her addiction many times, went to 12-step meetings, got a sponsor, and followed the program, she still was tempted, and she still slipped occasionally. Through her tears, she asks, "What can I do? I try so hard to control myself, and before I know it, I'm back in trouble again. It's almost as if I want to ruin my own life."

> Paul, *35,* a privileged lawyer in Beverly Hills, really wants to write a book, but he can't get himself to sit down and do it. "I know I can write. I've taken classes, and I really want to write this book, but it's almost as if I'll do anything to avoid sitting down at the computer and writing."

> Joe and Judy, a married couple in their 30s, want to have a loving, supportive relationship, but every discussion seems to turn into a fight about who's right or wrong or a bout of attacking and defending. Each time they have a fight, they spend several days hurt and separate. It's difficult to get anything accomplished in their life, their sexual connection is eroding, and so is their marriage.

Why It Happens

As I explained earlier, within the limbic brain system (toward the back of your head) resides your emotionally responsive, childlike mind—the part of your brain you were using as a young child, before the more complex, pre-frontal cortex had matured. Within this limbic system is a small brain organ called the *amygdala,* which has the extraordinary power to override your rational thinking brain in any situation perceived as an emergency. This is very important to survival. If a car is coming directly at you, you don't want to have to debate (or even think about) the issue before you jump out of the way. If you touch a hot stove, your amygdala will cause you to jump back before you are even aware of the pain. Your nervous system takes over and creates an instant response.

This amazing lifesaving system can become a problem when it takes over in non-threatening situations. When you feel out of control, your unthinking responses take over and cause you to respond in ways you wouldn't choose as an adult. These responses were learned before you were able to choose your reactions rationally.

As a small child, sucking your thumb or a bottle when you were anxious may have been effective, but as an adult, eating to calm your nerves can be problematic. The behavior and interaction styles you learned in childhood—how you deal with your time, money, religion, emotions, and all the other family styles of interaction examined in the last chapter—are programmed into your limbic brain, and, if stress or anxiety activate your amygdala, they can take over when you least expect it. So, if someone makes you angry, you find yourself reacting just as your raging father did (which you swore you'd never do). Or when stressful problems arise, perhaps you avoid talking about them and pretend nothing is wrong, the way your parents did. Understanding how you were programmed by childhood to talk too much, drink too much, overwork, get sick frequently, feel depressed or anxious, or overreact even when you know the situation doesn't warrant the overblown emotions is a key to making changes.

The Influence of Early Beliefs

As a small child, Lydia was severely neglected by her alcoholic mother and craved attention. She would do anything she could to get her mother to notice her. When she became a teenager, she got a lot of attention for her beauty. She learned she could get the attention she needed from boys by being sexually available. Her problems today stem from these learned patterns. As soon as she gets stressed and feels lonely or hurt, she has an uncontrollable urge to act out. Until she finds a way to reprogram her response to stress, her sexual compulsion will continue to be a problem.

Joe and Judy are both from families with divorced parents. Because as children they witnessed their parents arguing and the relationships breaking down and also because they never saw parents who worked out a relationship, they have few skills to help them work out their problems together. As soon as they get annoyed or frustrated with each other, they revert to their parents' fighting and struggling behavior.

Everyone has some leftovers from childhood, ranging from wonderful traditions to silly little annoying habits to major dysfunction. The same family who taught you problem patterns might have modeled a great sense of humor or how to comfort others. Each person's experience is different, even children from the same family. The key to getting in charge of your life is to find out how your limbic, childlike emotional brain was programmed from your childhood, deciding what you like and don't like about the programming, and then learning how to change the problem aspects.

The checklist exercise in the previous chapter was designed to help you see your family from a more objective viewpoint, differentiating your own family style from those of other families. In this exercise, you'll build on that, analyzing how much of your personal style today is related to the earlier, family style.

EXERCISE

Style Analysis

Once again, in your journal or notebook, list all the categories from your family styles exercise, as you did in the previous exercise. Leave some extra space for writing between the categories.

> Money
> Illness
> Health
> Sleep
> Food
> Religion
> Time
> Holidays
> Arguments
> Education
> Stress
> Cleanliness

Using your family styles categories for a reference, compare how you operate today in each style. Which ones do you do in a similar manner? Which are different? Are there categories in which you would like to do it differently than your family did, but you wind up doing what they did anyway?

You may want to take your time with this, coming back to it several times over a few days, to give yourself time to form a clear analysis.

In the same way that your family can program your emotional brain to behave in certain ways, it can also program you to be drawn to certain types of people.

Problem People

You have seen it many times—the woman who is attracted to abusive men, and dates or marries one after another; the man who seems to be searching for his mother; the friend who is always being taken advantage of in love relationships; or the office worker who reacts unreasonably to the same person over and over. Perhaps you've found that there are certain people to whom you are drawn, and others who you instantly dislike, for no apparent reason.

The limbic area of the brain (programmed by childhood experience) is in control here, too. When you react positively or negatively to certain people without reason or cause, your emotional-self is probably reacting to them because something about them reminds you of someone in your childhood.

To illustrate this, think of a person who just seems to upset you, annoy you, or repulse you, even if he or she has never done anything to you. Now, consider the members of your family who surrounded you in childhood. Does the upsetting person share the attributes of anyone from your past? Chances are, you'll see a connection.

Replicating Relationships

Family members who were significantly painful for you or loving toward you become "archetypes"—examples of character types we all recognize. Their behavior and your interactions with them can form patterns that influence your relationships today. Because these archetypes are familiar, they can feel comfortable, even if they're actually toxic for you. You can easily find yourself attracted to people who are similar to these archetypes and then interact with the new people according to old patterns. These archetypes are usually identified by gender, as in the following stereotypical examples:

> ➢ Dangerous, raging man

> ➢ Cold, critical woman

> ➢ Reliable, competent man

> ➢ Loving, affectionate woman

> ➢ Boyish, irresponsible man

> ➢ Helpless, naive woman

> ➢ Charming, violent man

> ➢ Teasing, seductive woman

Such attributes, character flaws, strengths, and weaknesses can be found in both men and women. People can be controlling, addicted, co-dependent (addicted to a toxic person), unreliable, dishonest, loving, supportive, trustworthy, affectionate, cold, mature, immature, or behave in many other ways that stand out and become a focus for the child mind.

If you had an aunt who was very loving toward you but had a drinking problem, you may (as an adult) find yourself drawn to women who are like her, or find yourself acting like her. If your father was angry and punishing, in adulthood you may find yourself attracted to angry men, or be very reactive toward them and unable to walk away.

EXERCISE

Reviewing Your Family Map

1. Get out your map of family members and their dysfunctions and attributes that you made in Chapter 1.

2. Focus on the relatives who were most important to you. Instead of thinking of them as the people they were, analyze their attributes.

3. Consider the people in your life today, especially difficult people or those with whom you have problems. Compare their styles and attributes with those of the people from your childhood.

4. If you find a correlation, a similar pattern, make a note. Who in your life today corresponds with a person from your past?

By examining your past and comparing it to now, you can trace the origins of your own behavior and attractions that you experience today. You can understand why you might be unreasonably suspicious toward someone who reminds you of a relative who tormented and teased you. Or you can see how you are equally unreasonably drawn to someone superficially similar to a family member who was warm, supportive, and understanding. Understanding these connections can help you to change the patterning that influences your current choices.

Whose Life Is It?

When your emotional, childlike limbic brain takes charge of your relationships and causes you to be attracted to familiar types of people, or to interact in familiar ways with them, it means that you are not really in charge of your own actions and choices. When life is uncertain in childhood and parents or other family figures are unreliable and unpredictable, a child learns to be vigilant, constantly watching others for clues. This child grows up to be an adult who is "outer-directed"—-that is, an adult who lives his or her life in response to others. Although such people are usually very good friends and wonderfully responsive and thoughtful, the problem is that they may not feel as if they know who they are, what they want, or who is in charge of their lives and decisions.

"Bonding is a strong emotional attachment that helps us want to be with one another, to help and protect one another, and to touch each other," writes Dr. Janov in *The Biology of Love.* "Those who did not bond very early on with their parents may well be condemned to a lifetime of broken, fragile, tenuous, and truncated relationships...if we see someone who cannot sustain long-term relationships, has one superficial relationship after another, and is stuck in a 'repetition compulsion,' we may postulate that he lacked close parental contact in infancy. We learn how to bond emotionally through early bonding, as simple as that sounds.

"A father who never shows happiness to see that baby, never responds with kindness to her cries is forming a new brain in the offspring...The stage is already set for later unhappiness and depression. She is now on a lifelong struggle to make the father happy to be with her—a fruitless effort...the woman can turn to men who are not impassioned with her so that she can struggle to make them like her.. .due to early trauma and its effects on the frontal area, the person cannot control herself and her needs. She will immediately act-out."

In *The Child Within,* John Bradshaw writes, "When caretakers are untrustworthy, children develop a deep sense of distrust...There is no way to be intimate with a partner who distrusts you...a child who never learned to trust confuses intensity with intimacy, obsession with care, and control with security."

In other words, difficult early relationships wind up running adult relationships. As adults, we are compelled to keep searching for the love we weren't able to get as children, and drawn to familiar people—those who remind us of family.

Early bonding and models can work in positive ways, too. When, as a child, you bond to relatives who are loving, supportive, trustworthy, and functional, you are attracted to similar people as adults. When you have learned healthy interaction skills as a child, your grownup relationships are much easier and more successful and fulfilling.

Realizing the power of early experience can be discouraging. You may be asking, "Once I have identified the source of my adult relationship problems in my childhood, am I condemned to keep repeating these patterns for my whole life?" "If I learned early to be outer-directed, will I never feel in charge of my own life?" Fortunately, the answer is no. As powerful as this early experience is, it is still possible to change the patterning in your subconscious, limbic brain.

Taking Charge

"The stages of human development are the same today as they were in the ancient times. As a child, you are brought up in a world of discipline, of obedience, and you are dependent on others," writes Joseph Campbell in *The Power of Myth.* "All this has to be transcended when you come to maturity, so that you can live not in dependency but with self-responsible authority, If you can't cross that threshold, you have the basis for neurosis."

Crossing the threshold from childhood dependency to adult autonomy is the key to growing up and out of dysfunction. Once you can recognize the childhood patterns and role models that run your unconscious reactions and responses to others, you can learn to change those patterns and make choices instead of reacting.

Reactive Versus Proactive

Children from dysfunctional families often grow up to live in a reactive way, responding to other people and to situations rather than proactively taking charge and making their own decisions. Handling life reactively means waiting until something happens and then responding to it, often in an intuitive or emotional fashion, rather than thinking through your response beforehand. It also means reacting in old ways, and reacting to people who remind you of family members. Reacting and responding are valuable options to have, but they can be problematic if you have no other choices.

Reacting

It is essential to be able to react when something unforeseen happens, and often there is no time to do more than respond emotionally or intuitively. Consider the following examples:

> ➤ Your 2-year-old child suddenly runs into the street. You immediately run after him, grab him, and drag him back onto the sidewalk before you know what you are doing.

> Without thinking, you swerve the wheel of the car you are driving to miss an object in the road.

> Someone in your office says, "Good morning. How are you?" and you respond automatically, "Fine thanks. How are you?"

> Your sister bursts into tears, and you put your arms around her and comfort her before you even know what's wrong.

> You touch a hot stove, and your hand seems to draw back by itself before you even register what's happening, and therefore the burn is not severe.

These are all appropriate reactive responses, and everyone uses this wonderful ability to act without thought or consideration every day. Most of the time it works. However, if your reactions are programmed by childhood events, you can find yourself in trouble.

> You become repeatedly and disastrously involved with people who are destructive (that is, loving a charming but hopeless alcoholic, being taken in by a smooth sales rep, saying "yes" to an irresponsible friend who wants to borrow your car).

> You spend money you can't afford (shopping when you're upset, loaning money to untrustworthy relatives, buying an extravagant car you can't afford).

> You behave in obsessive or addictive ways (overeating, getting drunk, working way too many hours for little pay, overscheduling yourself).

> You overreact to people, events, or circumstances, because they evoke early scenes and problems (having anxiety attacks, depression, rage, volatile relationships in situations others handle normally).

Being Proactive

Emotions are a good counterbalance for intellectual analysis of a given situation—because your emotional reaction to the person, situation, or event may make you aware of subtle subconscious clues you're picking up. However, when your emotional response is programmed from earlier times, you may not be truly reacting to what's going on now, but rather to what happened to you before. Emotional reaction is not a good substitute for rational decision-making.

One way to overcome childhood trauma, beliefs, and habits is to rationally evaluate your actions and reactions. When you take a moment to review what you're doing or about to do, or even to evaluate what you've already done, you aren't as likely to project your childhood experience onto today's events and people. Although learning to be proactive will not solve all your childhood leftovers, it will help minimize problems while you complete the rest of the work.

To avoid a purely emotional, programmed response, important decisions must be made with both the pre-frontal cortex and the limbic brain. That means, for best results, each significant decision you make should be considered intellectually as well as emotionally.

The Power of Proactive Choice

This advice is not new. There are many aphorisms and proverbs that express the folk wisdom of proactive decisions: "A stitch in time saves nine," "Look before you leap," "Before running mouth, be sure brain is engaged." These expressions exist in our culture (as well as other cultures) because they are lessons that many people have found to be true. Whether originated from the Bible, Shakespeare, Benjamin Franklin, or adopted from a popular song, movie, or play, the phrase catches on and is repeatedly used because it rings true.

We frequently fail to pay attention and think clearly enough to be proactive and decisive. You must be alert and aware to overcome your childhood programming, ignore your first impulse, and take decisive action. The good news is, it is not necessary to be proactive constantly—only when significant decisions need to be made. Being proactive now will save you a lot of work and hassle later.

For example, when building a house or a fence, it's the first layer of bricks that must be laid with extreme care, including lots of measuring, leveling, and so on, because all the other bricks laid will be determined by that first row.

Life decisions have a similar effect. Once the basic decisions are made, you can often relax and follow through on what you began without having to think every other aspect through as carefully. The initial decisions act as a blueprint for your future actions, giving you a plan to follow, so every act doesn't need to be so carefully thought thorough. Unfortunately, this same phenomenon works in a negative sense, also. If your initial decisions are not well thought out, everything you do later follows the original pattern and makes things worse.

Being proactive, then, is the first step to gaining control over your life. Once you decide to learn how to anticipate, evaluate, choose, and act wisely and effectively, you are on the path to making the kinds of decisions that are right for you at each phase of your life.

Steps to Proactive Decisions

In order to become in charge of your life and be less reactive, I teach my clients the following steps to learn to make more proactive decisions.

1. Anticipate the need to choose. Whenever possible, think ahead in your life—today, this week, this month, the coming year—and make plans for what you know you'll need to do. If a difficult situation is coming up, instead of just worrying about it, make some choices. If you need to make financial plans, or avoid getting involved in a family dispute, or simply to get your schedule under control, now is the time to think clearly and make your own choices.

2. Evaluate the situation and your options. Staying as calm as possible and keeping your focus on one problem to consider your options. What possible solutions could there be? If you have trouble coming up with enough choices, get some help from an expert or from other people you trust. Be willing to consider as many options as possible, even if some of them seem odd at first.

3. **Choose a reasonable course of action based on your evaluation.** Once you have explored enough options, a viable solution usually

presents itself. If there are no choices that seem obviously right to you, talk them over with a trusted adviser.

4. **Act on your choice.** A choice is not made until you act on it. Once you've decided your course of action, break it down into steps you can accomplish, and commit to doing the first step.

If you're used to making all your choices based on what other people want, do, or say, or not making choices until you're forced to, following these steps will be difficult at first. But making your own choices proactively is the beginning of your liberation from the past. If you find you can't do it, you may need to get help from a therapist or a support group.

Whose Problem Is It?

Young children are naturally egocentric. Because their experience of the world is so limited, they see everything from only their own point of view. They believe they're at the center of the universe, and everything revolves around them. Therefore, little Susie (or Johnny) assumes that whatever the adults are doing relates to her (or him). If Mommy is sad, Susie feels somehow responsible, and tries to help. If Daddy is tired and cranky, Johnny thinks he's done something wrong.

Because of their limited brain power and life experience, children use what we call "magical thinking" to understand the world. From what they observe, their limited knowledge, and by imitation, they guess what works, and the resulting behavior often seems strangely wise.

People find it amusing when a small child is described as "4 years old, going on 40." Small children can often seem wise and capable beyond their years. If a child has parents who are absent, incompetent, immature, or neglectful to the point that the child's well-being is neglected, the child often takes charge and tries to keep things together. He or she uses observation, imitation, experimentation, and pretending to solve problems and keep things together when the parents are not functioning well. Often this is an oldest child, who also takes responsibility for younger siblings and becomes a substitute parent for them as well as him- or herself. Eric Berne, M.D., the developer of Transactional Analysis theory, called such a child a "Little Professor." Robert Phillips, M.D., describes how this happens in his monograph, "Structural Symbiotic Systems":

When Tom reaches 24 months of age, he has had sufficient healthy parenting so that he is generally willing to relate to others pleasurably and to explore his small world with enthusiasm.

On a particular day he toddles into the kitchen where Mother is baking a cake for Father's birthday. His senses excited by the sight of Mother's busily relaxed body and by the combined smells of her body and bubbling chocolate, he looks up at Mother and smiles. She smiles in return and granted, he scurries happily to another room to explore, experiencing more stimulation from eye-catching and tactilely-differing objects. Soon he returns excitedly to the kitchen, bent perhaps on his first show-and-tell, alive with sensation and awareness.

But—what is this! There sits Mother in the corner of the kitchen, hunched over in a tense position and crying, with sharp edges on her sobs. Tom's world is suddenly disrupted— he whimpers and gets no response from Mother.

What has he done or not done to account for this catastrophe, Tom wonders in his small magical mind. Tom does not know and might never know that during his brief absence Mother received a telephone call from Father who angrily criticized her for omitting his habitual salami sandwich from the lunch-bag. Bewildered and fearful, Tom waits and waits and finally takes a desperate dare for survival. He awkwardly moves toward Mother, awkwardly extends his arm, and awkwardly pats her shoulder, uttering the magical words "I love you."

And with the suddenness of magic, Sobbing Beauty immediately comes to life again in Tom's world. Mother catches rapturous Tom up in her arms, wets his face with her redemptive sadness, and pronounces the words, which will become the curse of grandiosity, "You're my wonderful little man! I couldn't get along without you." Tom's small chest expands with pride, his head swells with self-righteousness, and he is immersed in a lethal mixture of liquids which someday might drown him—environmental tears, in combination with an internal bath of both adrenaline and acetyl-choline.

Little Tom has now taken over the role of comforting and parenting his mother. If this only happens sporadically, he will learn some useful skills and still have a mother who is capable when he needs her. But a child with a mother who is habitually helpless, perhaps drunk or incompetent, soon forms a habit of caretaking. Bright and resourceful children can do well enough at caretaking to get a lot of praise and gratification from their accomplishment.

Further problems arise when the Little Professor is smart enough to be successful at the caretaking. For such a child, caretaking and "acting as if" he or she knows what to do become strongly ingrained habits. A child with this background often grows up to be a highly competent, but stressed and anxious, adult. The anxiety is a result of pretending. No matter how successful and competent the person becomes, no matter what he or she achieves, it never seems real. The Little Professor feels like a child who's pretending to be grown-up.

Minister and licensed psychotherapist Denton Roberts vividly describes this feeling of "faking it" in *Able and Equal:*

> When I was a child I was a slow learner and considered myself less perceptive and bright than my peers. Since I decided this was a fact of life, I compensated by learning little techniques of "faking." With these techniques I kept up, passing from grade to grade, even though, as I well knew, I was not as bright as my friends.
>
> By the time I finished college I had managed to make the dean's list, which I credited not to intelligence, but to craftiness.. .Toward the end of graduate school, I confided to a friend that "I sure faked out Professor Graham—he gave me an A."...My friend retorted, "You must be pretty smart to fake out Professor Graham." His comment got through my firmly entrenched beliefs about my intelligence and I began to wonder—..."Could it be that I am intelligent and not just a good faker?"

Many years passed between deciding he was "slow" and realizing that being on the dean's list, achieving high intelligence test scores, and winning scholarships meant he was actually an authentically intelligent adult, and not just a child who was "faking."

Until this child in an adult's body does the work to separate his or her childlike-self from the past, bring it into the present, and acknowledge all his or her adult experience and expertise, he or she will feel as if someone else must be running his or her life.

Recovering from Little Professor syndrome is not difficult, once you realize you're behaving in this way. The key is to recognize your competence as an adult, and to learn to identify the difference between using your adult intelligence and using your childlike ability to "fake" what you're doing.

Guidelines for Using Grown-Up Thinking

1. **Pay attention to signals.** Notice when you feel anxious about what you're doing, especially if you're having anxiety attacks with rapid heartbeat or shortness of breath. This is a strong indication that you're in "Little Professor" mode. With practice, you can learn to identify the signals that you're anxious.

2. **Use logic.** Ask yourself some logical questions about what you're doing and feeling: Is there a good reason to be so nervous? What am I afraid of? What's the worst that could happen? How can I make sure I'm okay? Simply asking these questions, or questions about the facts—such as who, what, when, where, and why—will help you think more like a grown-up.

3. **Move into adult mode.** Remind yourself of all your adult experience and competence. Remember that you are not a child.

4. **Consider your reasoning.** Ask yourself why you're doing what you're doing. Can you explain it logically? If not, perhaps it's a reactive, rather than a rational, decision.

5. **Develop a plan.** Make a reasonable plan to accomplish whatever you want to do, break it down into steps, and stick to it. This will reduce the chances of being sidetracked by emotional reactions.

When you stay in your adult mode, you'll find that it's much easier to distinguish your true responsibilities from those that belong to others. You'll feel much more competent and much more in charge of your own life.

Achieving Maturity

Children who grow up in dysfunctional families often have trouble understanding and achieving emotional maturity, because the behavior of their childhood role models was not very mature. Such children often grow up in families where the boundary lines were confusing and become adults who don't understand how to differentiate their problems and responsibilities from those of others.

As long as you're a dependent child, your parents' problems are yours, because you may not be properly taken care of as long as your parent has a problem. Also, because as a child you have a tendency to take responsibility for everything that happens, you may decide that a parent's problem is all your fault. If Mom gets upset and angry, her children will assume that her anger is their fault. If she's cold and rejecting, the children not only feel unloved, but also unlovable. But Mother's coldness or anger has little to do with her children—it's a problem she has for other reasons—probably stemming from her own upbringing. As an adult, you can have more perspective about your mother and father and see that their character flaws are their own problems and existed before you came along.

When you understand that your parents' problems belong to them, and are not your fault or your responsibility to fix (although you may offer to help if you wish), you have achieved separation from that parent, and you've grown into an emotionally mature adult. The more control you have over your own thinking and your own actions, the less confused you become over whose responsibility is whose.

Even though your responses to the people around you are programmed in your early life by the role models and experiences within your family, you are not stuck with the result. By understanding the nature of your early beliefs, getting in charge of your emotional reactions, learning to view your family's style more objectively, and taking charge of your ability to make decisions, you can free yourself from endless repetition of dysfunctional family relationships.

Learning to recognize when your childhood beliefs and habits are taking over will help you avoid repeating the same problems over and over.

Chapter 5. The Inner Detective: Demystifying the Past

To the possession of the self the way is inward.
—Plotinus (A.D. 205—270)

Discovering how your early beliefs affect your adult relationships and learning to think before you react are helpful in taking charge of your life, but you may feel as if you're fighting yourself and struggling to control your reactions and emotional responses. If your emotional reactions don't really fit the events— whether you tend to overreact to certain situations or underreact to others—the cause is probably leftovers from your past.

The good news is that it's possible to find out what those causes are and to alleviate them. In my practice, clients often find they no longer need antidepressants, anti-anxiety drugs, or sleep medications once they resolve their leftover issues from childhood.

In order to figure out if childhood problems are still affecting your emotional reactions, it is necessary for you to become a special type of sleuth—an Inner Detective who, as famous literary detectives Sherlock Holmes or Hercule Poirot did, can find and observe clues and interpret what they mean.

Your Inner Detective

You have already begun creating an inner detective with the self-awareness and self-acceptance exercises in Chapter 2. Self-awareness and self-acceptance are the basic skills you need in order to observe the internal clues that will lead you to solving problems left over from your early childhood experience.

The biggest obstacle to most of my clients' healing and recovery is their inability to understand and accept their feelings and the emotional and behavioral clues that indicate where the problems lie. Most of us learn early that being too open with our feelings and thoughts is dangerous. It can lead to punishment, censure, ridicule, or hurt feelings. In some families, being open and honest about your feelings can be likened to giving other family members ammunition to use against you. Often in school settings, being emotionally open can be seen as being weak, and can lead to teasing, hurt feelings, or even physical danger. Therefore, you learn to repress and conceal your feelings and thoughts. Added to this, painful memories are also repressed, because you don't know what to do about them, and it's too painful to allow them to be in your awareness. Years of such suppression of feelings make it very difficult to open them up later on.

If you're overeating, overspending, overreacting, having anxiety attacks or temper tantrums, or otherwise out of control, the best way to get back in charge of your own behavior is to find out what feelings and thoughts you've repressed. To accomplish this, you need to develop the sleuthing skills of an Inner Detective.

Developing Detective Skills

Uncovering your inner secrets requires developing a set of detective skills similar to those a detective would use to uncover clues after a crime is committed. The difference is that the clues you are looking for are emotional and historical. You're part detective, part anthropologist, and the research site is your own mind. If you can uncover the hidden memories, thoughts, and feelings that are at the root of your problem, you can resolve the struggle between your emotional reactions and your rational intentions.

Detectives are not only skilled at their craft, but they also have specific character traits or attitudes that make them successful at deciphering clues. You can adapt these talents, skills, and traits to your own use, to search out the hidden thoughts and emotions behind your reactive and impulsive behavior.

These Inner Detective traits are: curiosity, persistence, observation, attentiveness, truthfulness, evidence-seeking, reliability, consistency, and a questing nature. Each of these traits can be learned, or are attributes you already possess but have not used internally before. Imagine any detective, fictional or real, and see how these traits would be expressed by that detective.

Curiosity

Without curiosity, no detective could be very successful. Curiosity is the quality of wanting to know, to ask all the questions. If you apply it to your emotional secrets, you'll want to know what's going on. There is nothing more interesting than what is going on in your own mind and emotions.

Diane, a client who was cut off from knowing what she was feeling, told me that she had been riding her bicycle and had suddenly burst into tears "for no reason." I explained that emotions always have a reason, even if it's not related to what's going on right now. Diane had to learn to be curious about her own emotions. We talked about how Diane would feel if she were riding with a friend, and the friend had suddenly burst into tears for some unknown reason. Diane agreed that she would be intensely curious and concerned, and she became aware that her lack of interest in her own feelings was not appropriate. She started to take an interest in her feelings and what might be upsetting her. It took a while, but she now pays attention when she has an emotional reaction, even a small one. This curiosity has led to Diane's knowing a lot more about herself and beginning to solve some of her relationship problems.

Being curious about your emotions and thoughts will lead you to understanding and to explanations of things that, until now, have been mystifying. What's underneath your depression, your anxiety, your impulsive behaviors, your out-of-control emotions? Getting interested in what you think and feel, as you would be in what is going on with your friend, your spouse, or your children, is the key to finding the information that will help you improve your relationship with yourself and with others.

Persistence

Persistence is the quality of not giving up, hanging in there, keeping on keeping on until you find out what you want to know. If someone asks you what you feel or think, the instant answer is often, "I don't know." But to a detective, it's not an acceptable answer. Only you know your own thoughts and feelings. "I don't know" is the equivalent of "I give up," and a detective doesn't quit. Persistence means not giving up on yourself. Not caring what you feel means not caring that you are alive. You wouldn't do that to a friend, so don't treat yourself as if you're not important. The self-awareness exercise in Chapter 2 is designed to help you understand your feelings— but only if you use it persistently.

It's common for a client to do an exercise in therapy, get excellent results, but then fail to practice it regularly, because new behavior is uncomfortable and unfamiliar. Persist in doing the exercises and ask others to help remind you. Striving to understand yourself will result in success, just as persisting in the search for *all* the evidence helps a detective solve a case.

Observation

Extraordinary powers of observation are a hallmark of the effective detective. Observation is the key to noticing important clues. The detective who sees the tiny details—as exemplified by Sherlock Holmes, Hercule Poirot, Nancy Drew, or the TV detectives Columbo and Monk—is the most successful. Becoming observant about your own patterns, reactions, and feelings will also help you be successful at unearthing the hidden clues. Pay attention to patterns: For example, what happens just before you become anxious or upset? These patterns contain clues about your "triggers" or what brings up the hidden emotions and memories. Observe your physical body sensations—where do you feel the emotion in your body? That spot in your body will be a great resource for uncovering many important clues. Detectives often go undercover, where they become "participant-observers" in a situation where they need to get information. That means, they infiltrate the gang, the drug dealer's group, or the terrorist group to observe their actions and find out their plans. Psychologists and anthropologists also use this "participant/observer" technique to do research. You can use this tool in your own life, by consciously "stepping aside" and observing what's happening in you and around you as objectively as you can. The more you can observe yourself objectively, the more you will learn to be aware of what you're doing.

Attentiveness

The attentive detective is not only observant and persistent, but also alert and aware. Attentiveness, being fully present, means you're observant and thinking clearly. Being attentive all the time is impossible, and not even necessary. However, when emotional clues are present, it can make a big difference. If you learn what triggers your emotional reactions, and to recognize the clues that your emotions are taking over, your attentiveness will help you learn what you need to know to take control. If you have a tendency to avoid your feelings, you've learned to be somewhat numb and inattentive. Paying attention whenever your feelings are involved will increase your ability to understand those feelings, and what triggers them, and to uncover the hidden beliefs and leftover issues of the past.

Truthfulness

At times, a great detective may mislead other people (particularly the villain) to get information. But in solving a case, the only thing that works for a great sleuth is the truth. In the words of *Dragnet's* Joe Friday, they focus on "Just the facts, Ma'am." Successful detectives are always truthful with themselves and about the facts. It might be quicker and easier to solve a case by interpreting the facts (finding the truth) in the light of your desired outcome. Lazy, incompetent, or dishonest detectives can do this and reach the wrong result. A top-notch detective, however, is scrupulous in looking for the truth about the evidence. It is just as important to seek the truth when you're an inner detective. Rather than settling for an easy answer to why you're afraid or angry, keep looking until you know the truth. Christians learn that the truth is quite easily recognized because it "will set you free." It is a very useful idea whether you're religious or not. Emotional truth does set you free—a type of freedom we psychologists call "release." Clients often say, "So that's what it was! I never saw it that way before!" when they uncover the truth. Uncovering the truth about why you're afraid, angry, hurt, or sad produces various types of release:

> ➢ A feeling of "Aha!" indicating a new understanding of the situation.

> ➢ A sigh of relief.

> ➢ A flood of tears.

> ➢ A burst of laughter.

> ➢ "Wow!" So that's what that's about!

Evidence-Seeking

Curiosity and truthfulness are crucial to good detective work. There's another related quality that's equally important. Reporters call it "a nose for news." Scientists call it "scientific curiosity." Great detectives have an eagerness to find the facts, to learn what happened. Evidence-seeking is more directed than curiosity and less strict than truthfulness. It's similar to the energy that motivates people to solve puzzles or keeps them eagerly paging through a murder mystery or glued to a reality crime show on TV. Once you get interested in seeking evidence, you'll find your own subconscious is far more fascinating and interesting than any novel.

Reliability

How would a detective get hired to solve crimes if he wasn't reliable? A lot of detective work has to do with making connections that can supply information. In order to establish trust with such connections, a detective must be reliable. To find out what information is hidden in your subconscious, childlike emotional mind, you need to gain its trust in a similar way. By being consistent and reliable about following up on the clues, you'll find that the truth is more and more available to you.

Consistency

A good detective has an organized way of doing a search and follows that process in the same way each time. Detectives are consistent in this way because it means they don't skip steps or miss valuable clues. Consistently and methodically searching for your hidden beliefs and feelings will help you be more effective at finding out what you need to know.

Questing Nature

For super detectives, their vocation is more than just a job. Sherlock Holmes is not just working for a living; he feels his work is his life's purpose, and he dedicates a huge portion of his life, money, time, and energy to the task. Understanding that your search for the early experiences, archaic ideas and beliefs, and leftover feelings that are at the root of your tension today is a life quest that will have incredibly powerful rewards for you.

These are the attributes you'll need to uncover the evidence of your emotions and your history. You can create your own versions of all these qualities, and use them to help you search through your past experience, your memories and your emotions for the truth that will set you free from out of control behavior and feelings.

Searching for Clues

When you find evidence that early issues are affecting your current life, it's necessary to search for the details of the early events and issues that are still affecting you. Using your detective skills of curiosity, persistence, observation, attentiveness, truthfulness, evidence-seeking, reliability, consistency, and a questing nature, you can do the following exercises and uncover the clues that will make it possible to clear up your confusion. By learning how to "track down" dysfunctional beliefs by recognizing the telltale signs, following the clues, and confronting the early traumatic scenes that did the damage, you'll learn to relate directly to yourself and get in charge of your reactions, habits, and beliefs.

For example, if you find that you have anxiety attacks or other evidence of tension, such as a tense feeling in your stomach, chest, or back, and you understand that such feelings are evidence of problems from your past, you can use this evidence to track down the early problem and diffuse it. If you do this consistently, your anxiety and tension will fade, and you'll be able to clear up any new tension quickly on the spot. This is how I teach my clients to find the source of emotions in their body sensations.

EXERCISE

Tracking Body Sensations

1. **Find your tension spot**. Sit in a comfortable place, where you won't be interrupted. Close your eyes, and take a few moments to focus on your body. Using your curiosity, attentiveness, and powers of observation, mentally go over your body to find the place where tension or upset seems to be most strongly concentrated. You may discover tension or tightness in your chest, stomach area, head, neck or shoulders, arms, legs, or back. If you have trouble locating it, remember a time when you were upset, and you should be able to feel where the upset is lodged in your body. When you have found the spot, put your awareness on the part of your body. If you discover several tension spots, choose the one that feels most intense and begin there. If you discover none, try focusing on your chest area. Focus your attention there and visualize soothing, relaxing warmth beginning to surround and penetrate it and ease the discomfort. After a few moments you will probably feel the tension let go a little. To help yourself feel the warmth better, gently place your hand there.

2. **Be a good listener.** Place your attention where your hand is, and say gently to your spot (to increase the chances that your emotional attitude is helpful and caring) "I'm ready to hear what you have to tell me." Listen, for a while, to what your subconscious inner self has to say, holding your attention on the spot. Your spot will communicate to you in words, images, or physical feelings, whichever come naturally to your subconscious. Use your detective skills of attentiveness, observation, and persistence to decipher the information. Do not censor or reject any thought that comes into your mind now. Just pay gentle attention, and allow whatever images, ideas, physical sensations, or thoughts you discover to surface into your awareness.

3. **Allow plenty of time**. Allow enough time (about 10 minutes, in the beginning) for the images and/or sensations to emerge from within you. Image you're a detective staking out a crime scene to watch for clues—your questing nature, combined with persistence and evidence-seeking, will help you have the patience to wait for the information to emerge. When you begin to get images and sensations, don't argue or agree with them, just let them come. If your inner voice says, "I don't know," or "I don't want to tell," say something along the lines of, "I'd really like to hear, I know I've neglected you, but now I realize you're there, and I'd like to hear what you have to say." Or just sit quietly and patiently for a while, to demonstrate that

you are willing to listen. Accept whatever information you get, however meaningless or silly it seems. You probably have an old childhood belief that your feelings aren't important, so counteract that by assuming what you get is meaningful, even if you don't understand it.

You may get physical sensations: warmth, cold, your pulse beating, a tightening, or a relaxing. You may receive symbolic images: a wall, a knot, fire, yourself as a child, religious or fictional characters, or wise teachers. You may remember early scenes from your own history. You may just "hear" your inner self talk in a matter-of-fact way. Whatever you receive, maintain a "this is interesting—tell me more" attitude, as you would if a friend were telling you about his or her inner secrets. This friendly interest will help the information flow faster and prevent the blockage caused by criticism or argument.

You are creating a new awareness of yourself and your feelings as you do this, so allow yourself enough time for this new attitude and method, and be as open to learning new things from your inner self as you can. What you discover may be simply interesting or it may be very emotional. Be patient with the process—the rewards are worth it.

4. **Begin a mutual dialogue.** After receiving whatever your trouble spot has to share with you, you can begin a dialogue. Offer suggestions, but don't argue right or wrong. Your objective is to become aware of and understand the issue that your inner self is trying to bring to your attention. Try not to attack or discount what you learn, and strive for understanding. Your subconscious speaks in its own language, the language of your dreams and intuition. It may take you a while to understand it. Keep in mind that this is a part of you "talking," and you already know everything you need to understand what your spot is saying.

Learning to listen to your inner voice is much like prayer or meditation—keeping an open mind, focused here on your tension spot. Your quest is to find out what in your memory, feelings, or subconscious mind is troubling you and to work with these feeling and beliefs until they are resolved and dispelled.

5. **Repeat for proficiency.** The more you make contact with your trouble spot and practice listening and dialogue, the easier this exercise will get. After repeating it four or five times, you will find that you can "check in"

with your spot more easily. After 20 times, you'll be able to do it on a moment's notice, without closing your eyes, and even while you're doing other things. In this situation, persistence and a questing nature pays off. The ability to be quickly aware of your inner prompting makes it possible for you to deal with your feelings, impulses, and reactions before they cause you to act rashly. You'll then be able to rethink your actions and your responses to other people and make rational choices.

Reactions to Other People

Difficulty in relationships with people is one of the most frequent leftovers of growing up in a dysfunctional family. If you are reactive to a certain stimulus—for example, you grew up with a punishing father, so you overreact to anyone in authority over you—you will have repeatedly similar trouble with a certain type of people, as we discussed in Chapter 4. You can easily be attracted to people who are similar to adults from your childhood: If you grew up with a depressed mother or a workaholic father, you may find yourself gravitating toward that type of personality, because it feels familiar. The problems you encounter with that familiar type of person may not emerge until you're already bonded and involved.

Mirrors and Teachers

You can learn a lot about yourself and also acquire many useful life skills by looking at the people who upset you from a different perspective. Seeing difficult people as reflections of your psychological/emotional issues can be amazingly valuable in your search for inner clues.

Psychologists know that we have a tendency to relate to people similarly to the way we related in our childhood. If you grew up trying to get a cold, withdrawn parent to love you, you could chase after cold, unavailable people as a grown-up. We also relate to others as we relate to ourselves. For example, if you're very critical of yourself, you'll tend to criticize others, and you'll also be drawn to people who are critical. You will not really notice (or you'll make excuses for) criticism that would make someone else cringe and avoid the person who said it.

To see difficult people as useful mirrors, you must step back and look at your interaction with them as a source of information about yourself. Knowing what upsets you, and what you want from that person, you can infer the emotional need or problem behind the dynamics.

The following exercise will show you how to view people from a different angle, to use the very people who upset you as a reflection of the internal dynamics behind your struggles. You can use this mirror technique the way Sherlock Holmes uses his magnifying glass to make clues visible.

EXERCISE

Mirrors and Teachers

1. **List problem people.** Make a list of people with whom you have had problems in the recent past. You can use the list you created in Chapter 4 from the exercise for reviewing your family map. Choose the family members who are still presenting problems, and add to it other people who are difficult but aren't related.

2. **Choose a mirror.** Select one of the most difficult people on the list, and think about your interaction with that person. What do you want from him or her? Do you want to be understood? To be respected? To be left alone? To be appreciated? To be cared about?

3. **Relate it to yourself.** Now consider how to give to yourself what you want from the other person. If you want to be left alone, do you leave yourself alone? If you want to be trusted, do you trust yourself? If you want to be heard, do you listen to your own self? If you want to be important, are you important to you?

4. **Change your self-treatment.** Practice treating yourself the way you would want to be treated by the person in question. For example, if you are angry because this person doesn't treat you with respect, consider what it would mean to treat yourself with respect, and change your behavior toward yourself accordingly. If you're upset because the person doesn't listen to you, spend some time every day listening to yourself.

5. **Learn new skills.** Think about the dynamics between the difficult person and yourself, and what you need to learn that would improve the relationship. Perhaps you need to learn not to take what is said too seriously. Perhaps you need to learn to set boundaries, or to handle other people's anger more effectively. Make a list of new skills you could learn that would improve your ability to deal better with this type of individual. On your list, note where you think you could learn the skills you need. From a friend? With a therapist? From books? Some of the exercises in the rest of this book may give you what you need.

6. **Do your** part. Take responsibility for your part of the relationship. Keeping in mind that no one can struggle with you if you don't struggle back, consider what you need to do to remove yourself from the relationship problem. Remember: No matter what's going on, you have control over your own actions—you can choose not to participate in any situation that is destructive or counterproductive.

Helpful Techniques for Diffusing Difficult Relationships

The following two techniques can help you deal with difficult people and control your involvement when a relationship proves difficult to handle because the other person's behavior is truly out of control or because behaviors that were acceptable to your childhood family are no longer acceptable to you. Behaviors such as:

➢ Drunkenness or a drugged state

➢ Abusive or obnoxious language

➢ Rage and yelling

➢ Physical violence toward people or objects

➢ Inappropriate sexual innuendoes and advances

➢ Mean and belittling comments, either to you or behind your back

➢ Socially unacceptable traits, such as displays of bigotry or racism

➢ Embarrassing behavior of any kind (especially if repeated)

Technique 1. Someone Else's Family

When a family member is difficult, you can learn to treat him as if he were from the family of someone you care about, and not your own. After all, if you were with a friend's family, and someone did something odd, you'd just ignore it, and you wouldn't let yourself be drawn into family squabbles. You'd just be polite and pleasant, for your friend's sake. This allows you to get some distance from the person's bad behavior and not react to it. For example, you can treat your own parents as if they were a friend's parents or your sister or brother as though they were someone else's sibling. Thinking about the relationship in this new way will give you the distance and perspective you need to be less reactive to the problem person. It will help you to see that there's no need to be angry, afraid, or dependent on the family member—instead, you can keep your emotional distance.

Technique 2. Adult Time-Out

If someone behaves badly in your presence, giving that adult a "time-out" is a powerful and subtle way of fixing the problem. Modern parents use a *time-out* to discipline small children. The child is sent to a corner, or a room, to think about his or her behavior. An adult variation of the time-out works as well on any anyone—in your family, at work, at school, or among your friends—who is acting childish or misbehaving. All you need to do is become very distant and polite around the person who is not treating you well. No personal talk and interaction, no joking, no emotion. Be very polite, so the person cannot accuse you of being unpleasant, mean, or rude. There is no need to explain what you are doing: The problem person will get the message from your behavior—which is much more effective. If you've never tried this, you'll be amazed at how effective becoming polite and pleasant, but distant, can be. Most of the time the other person's behavior will immediately become more subdued around you and often much more caring. Eventually, that person may ask you what's wrong, or why you've changed, and at that point (and only at that point) you have an opportunity to tell him or her, what the problem behavior is and why you don't like it. Learning to put obnoxious people in a time-out right at the beginning of unpleasant behavior can make it unnecessary to use tougher tactics at all.

Demystifying the Past through Therapy

Even the best detective can't always solve every case by himself. If your childhood leftovers are giving you problems, coming up in your relationships, or preventing you from doing what you want, you may need some help. If you find that any of the exercises in this book bring up old upsetting experiences, or if there are people you cannot handle or problems you cannot solve, the smartest thing to do is to get therapy. A competent licensed therapist will help you understand the meaning of upsetting memories, stop disturbing nightmares, and help you learn to manage your emotions if you are having trouble. The following guidelines will help you choose a therapist who is right for you.

Guidelines for Finding and Using Therapy Wisely

When to look for a therapist

> ➤ You have problems that you can't solve by yourself or talking to friends and family.

> ➤ You cannot control such behaviors as temper tantrums, alcohol or drug addiction, painful relationships, anxiety attacks, or depression.

> ➤ You have serious difficulties communicating in your relationships.

> ➤ You have sexual problems or sexual dysfunction that does not go away by itself.

> ➤ You have violent or abusive relationships.

> ➤ You have a general, pervasive unhappiness with your life.

Where to look for a therapist

Finding a counselor is easy. Licensed counselors of every sort exist everywhere, and they can be found in the phone book or via an online search. Finding the *right* counselor is harder, but critically important to your success in counseling. As with lawyers, plumbers, or doctors, the quality of counselors and therapists can vary. You need a referral or recommendation of an effective, suitable, and experienced counselor in your area. There are several sources that are good, depending on what's available to you.

Advertising This is the least dependable source to find the right counselor, because you usually cannot tell from an ad whether the counselor has had the proper training for your issues or whether you'll feel good about him or her. If you don't have a referral from someone you know, you can interview therapists by phone (using the guidelines on page 126), and choose the best one.

Hotlines Even if you are not suicidal or a domestic violence or rape victim, you can call a local hotline and most of them will refer you to a counselor or clinic in your area. These hotlines often know the counselors personally—

you can ask how they screen their referrals. Hotline staff are well trained and know the resources in your area. Look in the front pages of your phone book for a list of hotlines.

Internet search If you have access to online searching, you can find a lot of therapists online. Look for online groups that specialize in your issues, such as depression, anxiety, addiction, or relationships.

Nonprofit professional associations Associations of counselors and therapists can refer you to a therapist in your area that has met the organization's qualifications. This is especially important if you live in an area where counselors are not licensed. Try The Association for Humanistic Psychology *(www.ahp.oig)* , The American Association for Marriage Family Therapists *(www.camft.org),* or The American Psychotherapy Association *(www.americanpsychotherapy.com).* Such nonprofit organizations are also listed in the phone book and directory assistance, with branches in major cities.

Referrals from friends The best source for a good counselor is probably referrals from friends who have seen a counselor and can tell you firsthand that he or she is competent, friendly, and effective. Any counselor who is recommended by someone you know will most likely be your best bet.

Find a counselor who is supportive and understanding and with whom you are comfortable. If you don't, you will be less open and forthcoming about your problems, and your counselor cannot be helpful. To see a counselor and withhold information is the equivalent of taking your car to a mechanic and giving him false information about what's wrong. The counselor, like the mechanic, is liable to focus on fixing the wrong thing.

A good, knowledgeable counselor will be informative and helpful when you call to ask for information and will gladly explain the counseling process to you. He or she will also be willing to answer any questions you have about the counseling process at any time and will lead you step by step through the procedure.

What to expect from a counseling session. Knowing how a session should go will help you maximize the benefits of counseling and also prevent potential problems.

So far, so good. You've decided to seek counseling, found a referral, and now you're facing the moment of truth: calling for an appointment. There is no need to be afraid of this. If this is a counselor who's been personally recommended, you have an excellent chance that you've found someone good. If you got the name from other sources, then it's up to you to check your chosen professional out. Here's how to go about **it:**

Interviewing a Therapist

What you need to know

Normally, you will call the counselor first for an appointment. If you know in advance what you'd like to find out about the counselor, you can take charge of the phone conversation, and make sure you find out as much about him or her as he or she does about you.

There are several things you will want to know in advance:

> **Expertise.** Is the counselor licensed? What is his or her area of expertise? Does he or she work with depression, anxiety, recovery, or whatever issue you want to focus on?

> **Price.** How long is a session? What is the rate; is there a sliding scale?

> **Payment.** Will he take a check? Does he take your insurance? Are there charges for filling out insurance papers? Do you pay in advance and have insurance reimburse you, or does he get paid by insurance directly? Some counselors today even take credit cards.

> **Hours.** Does she recommend how often you come in, or can you set the frequency of visits according to your needs, finances, and work schedule? Does she see clients nights or weekends?

> **Duration** Does this counselor do long-term or short-term therapy? Not very long ago, most therapy was very intensive and took years to complete, but today's therapy techniques can handle your immediate problems in just a few sessions, especially if you have done the exercises in this book and already have an understanding of what you might need to work on.

Phone Interview

If a receptionist or a secretary answers when you phone a therapist, ask to speak directly with the counselor. Most often, the therapist will be "in session"—counseling someone—when you call and will not be able to take your call immediately, but he can call you back if you leave a message that says *specifically* when you're available ("after 6 in the evening" or "Saturday all day," for example) or you can find out when he is available to take calls and call back then. Some counselors will offer a free or low-cost initial interview in which you can ask questions and find out details for little or no charge. Keep calling and interviewing therapists until the previous questions have been answered to your satisfaction, and then make an appointment.

The First Session

When you go into the office, you will probably be given forms to fill out, as in a medical doctor's office. There are several reasons for this:

1. To get the necessary information for filling out insurance forms (name, address, social security number, date of birth, nature of problem, name and number of your medical doctor).

2. To learn some facts about you that will help in counseling (family history, marital history, any previous hospitalizations for mental illness, current medications, or previous therapy).

3. To begin a file the therapist will keep on you and your progress.

Although it is rare, these records can be subpoenaed by a court, so don't answer any questions you find uncomfortable. Give your answers to those questions verbally to the counselor instead, and explain that you don't want them written down, because you want your privacy protected. Don't be too worried about this; your counselor will not divulge information unless a court requires him to, but you have a right to know what is and is not protected information.

Once the forms are filled out, your counselor will see you in her office and the session will begin. The first session is called an *intake session,* which is an initial interview. If you have a clear idea of what the problem is before you go in, your counselor will be more effective. You will probably be asked what is wrong, what you have tried to do to fix it, and how you think it should be resolved. A good counselor will be neutral, helpful, and may offer suggestions, even give you "homework" (an exercise to do between sessions), but he should not impose his beliefs or ideas on you.

If you felt good about your counselor on the phone, this session should verify that you are in knowledgeable hands. If, in the first few sessions, you can see that the therapy will be helpful, and you're learning new things, you're probably in the right place.

Therapist Statement of Ethics
This is the statement of ethics published by the American Psychotherapy Association, for their members to hand out to their clients. Other professional associations have similar codes. I reproduce it here to give you an idea of ethical counseling behavior.

As a psychotherapist:

➤ I must first do no harm.

➤ I will promote healing and well-being in my clients and place the client's and public's interests above my own at all times.

➤ I will respect the dignity of the persons with whom I am working, and I will remain objective in my relationships with clients and will act with integrity in dealing with other professionals.

➤ I will provide only those services for which I have had the appropriate training and experience and will keep my technical competency at the highest level in order to uphold professional standards of practice.

➤ I will not violate the physical boundaries of the client and will always provide a safe and trusting haven for healing.

➤ I will defend the profession against unjust criticism and defend colleagues against unjust actions.

> ➤ I will seek to improve and expand my knowledge through continuing education and training.

> ➤ I will refrain from any conduct that would reflect adversely upon the best interest of the American Psychotherapy Association and its ethical standard of practice.

A counselor or therapist who adheres to this or a similar code will behave ethically and be an effective help in your search to demystify your past.

Whether you do your search to demystify your past by yourself or use the help of a therapist, you'll find that the information concealed in your own mind is fascinating and valuable. In the next chapter, we'll examine the patterns you learned in the past and how to change them.

Chapter 6   Changing Old Patterns: Re-Creating Yourself

Habit is habit, and not to be flung out of the window by any man, but coaxed downstairs a step at a time.
—Mark Twain

Patterns, patterns. Human beings are hardwired to seek out patterns and operate according to them. Every waking moment we are bombarded by overwhelming floods of data, infinite numbers of choices, confusing and conflicting information. Sheer survival depends upon your brain being able to sort through all of this every minute. The ingenious solution, built right into your brain and nervous system, is the ability to operate according to patterns.

The Power of Pattern

Your brain automatically searches and identifies many kinds of patterns. Patterns of sight mean that you can identify the chair from the table, the dining room from the bedroom, whether you see them in their three-dimensional form, or see a photograph, or even see the drawing created by your 6-year-old. Van Gogh's or Picasso's table is recognizable even though the perspective is skewed and the colors are strange. It still fits the pattern of table. Kinesthetic patterns mean you can reach for a utensil, pot, or dish in the kitchen without even looking where you reach, or grab your toothbrush in the bathroom before you're really awake. A combination of kinesthetic and visual patterns means you can drive the familiar drive to work without even thinking about it—and if you get a new job or move, you'll find yourself taking the old route if you don't pay attention.

The stress of paying attention is one of the major reasons why patterns are important. Research shows that moving to a new home is one of the most stressful experiences you can have, right up there with the death of a loved one. This doesn't appear to make sense, because moving to a new home is usually a desirable thing, until you think about patterns. All those kinesthetic, visual patterns have suddenly changed—the pots, dishes, and your toothbrush (not to mention the bathroom) are all in different places. So is the furniture. You're tripping over chairs that seem to be in the wrong places. You have to think every minute of the drive to work, because the route is unfamiliar. Each of these changed patterns represents a lot of stress.

When you're operating within old, familiar patterns, you don't need to think about what you're doing. Your body is wired to do familiar things without having to think about them. This leaves your mind free to wander and to de-stress.

Learning New Patterns, Changing Old Ones

As I write this, I'm touch-typing. I don't have to think about the spelling of the words or which finger hits which key. There was a time, of course, when I couldn't type even one word without hunting and pecking for each letter, but (in the beginning) painstaking practice and repetition, and now many years of experience, mean that I can even talk to someone else while I type. Repetition and practice made the patterns part of my consciousness.

If you want to change a habit (for example, to develop a habit of wearing your car seat belt), you develop a pattern that incorporates the change: I'll get in my car, put the key in the ignition, fasten the seat belt, *and then* start the car. At first, you may even need a written note to remind you of the pattern, but if you consistently follow your new routine, it will be a pattern in a week or two. If you do it for several weeks, it will become ingrained enough to feel automatic— you won't need to think about it at all. Changing even really tough patterns, such as smoking, is possible if you break it down into each smoking habit you have (after dinner, at work, hanging out with friends), develop a replacement pattern for each one (chew mint gum after dinner; take a short, brisk walk during work breaks; hang out in nonsmoking places with friends), and follow each new pattern consistently until all are changed. Having something different to focus on, makes the psychological withdrawal easier.

Emotional Patterns

Emotional and relationship patterns work in similar ways. When we can relate to others in recognizable patterns, we feel more comfortable, even if the patterns are toxic. Psychologists have long known that people will choose what's familiar, even if it's painful, over whatever is different and unknown.

Early Patterns in Action

We learn family patterns very early in life without understanding whether those patterns are healthy or not. Because the habits and patterns are established so young, they just seem "normal" or "automatic" to us, rather than something we can choose. Clients often say, "I can't help it. I've always done it that way," when I ask them to change some destructive pattern such as having temper tantrums or letting people take advantage of them. It's partially true. They can't help it *until* they understand it's a pattern—and what they need to do to change that pattern.

Perhaps you grew up with an angry parent and keep choosing angry, abusive partners. Or if your family map contains a lot of drinkers, perhaps you wind up with alcoholic mates, because you don't recognize excessive drinking when you see it, so it looks normal to you.

If your conversations with people often get out of hand and turn into arguments, or you find yourself saying yes to things you don't want to do or agree with, or you frequently feel anxious and nervous around others, your early patterns are probably at work.

The good news is that you are not stuck with your emotional and relationship patterns. Just as physical habits can, emotional habits can be changed.

Tools for Changing Old Patterns

Once they're ingrained enough, early patterns become belief systems. That is, if, as a child I had temper tantrums and no one helped me learn how to control them, I grow up believing I am a person with a bad temper, I can't help it, and it's just who I am.

Sarah is very upset because she has very nearly ruined the relationship she has with someone she loves very much. She has been too reactive, never giving her partner a moment's peace, demanding whatever she wants, and getting very angry if her demands aren't met. She's finally stopped blaming everyone else, and she sees that her behavior is a problem. "But what can I do? I've always been this way; it's how I am." With guidance, she goes back to her early childhood, when she used to lie on the floor and kick and scream, and she says everyone just ignored her—they did nothing to help her.

I asked her to identify what it is she is angry about.

"I hate school. I don't want to go, so I get angry about stupid things. I'm angry that the socks I want to wear are dirty."

"What happens?"

"I just lie on the floor and scream. No one pays any attention to me. They pretend it's not happening."

"Did you go to school that day?"

Sarah looks up, astonished and wide-eyed to realize her tantrum got rewarded. "No, I didn't. I screamed for a while, then went to my room."

Sarah has just begun to realize that her temper is just a learned habit— something that worked for her (although in a toxic way) and got her what she wanted as a child. She did know that her parents were instilling this toxic habit in her, but she never before realized that they let her win by ignoring the tantrum and also the issue. Each time she had an angry outburst, as a child and as an adult, she reinforced the habit. The following diagram shows how the cycle of reinforcement works.

The Dysfunctional Habit Cycle

1. Early learning. We learn whatever we learn, at first, because it works in some way. When the family environment is dysfunctional, what works might mean whatever gets us instant gratification. This "successful" result or reward for the behavior might not look good to anyone not within the family system. In fact, it often looks very destructive. A "reward" in this dysfunctional environment, might be:

> *Avoiding abuse:* Complying, hiding, lying, leaving, blaming, anything to shift attention from oneself and avoid the explosion of abuse.

➢ *Provoking abuse:* If it's not possible to avoid the abuse, sometimes children learn to set the abuser off, because they can survive the abuse, and afterward they get a period of safety and relative peace.

➢ *Avoiding conflict:* Being a "good" boy or girl (complying and denying self), peace-making, walking on eggshells (behaving with exaggerated care, to avoid problems), seduction (using charm and sexuality to manipulate), or falsely agreeing rather than setting off a fight.

➢ *Hyper-vigilance:* This is a highly anxious state, usually found in violent, chaotic families, where, in order to survive, the child feels he or she needs to know what's about to happen at all times. This child watches the adults intently and continuously, always terrified that something awful is going to happen. Anxiety attacks and asthma are a side effect of this, and they might be rewarded with lots of attention, also.

➢ *Causing conflict:* If the only attention and recognition you get is when there's a fight, a child will learn to create fights for attention.

➢ *Getting sympathy:* The best way to get positive attention in the family might be to be sick or very sad or to have a problem.

➢ *Silence:* The only safe thing to do might be to shut down and become very quiet.

➢ *Drama:* Often creating a scene or an overblown problem, making mountains out of molehills, might be the best way to get attention and praise.

➢ *Solving problems:* Often, a child will be the member of the family who solves everyone's problems—except his or her own. That child's intelligence and! or ability is often praised, but he or she usually feels deprived and neglected.

2. Rote behavior, not thinking. Once a behavior is learned and then enforced until it becomes habitual, the child no longer has to think or guess what to do. He or she just waits for the clues and does the behavior without thinking or really realizing it. People operating within these dysfunctional patterns often feel mystified, confused, and helpless. The pattern is now running the person.

3. Negative results. Of course, in addition to achieving immediate gratification of the neurotic need, such patterns create a lot of negative results: fighting, rage, violence, abuse, chaos, paranoia, isolation, anxiety, depression, and passive behavior. People in dysfunctional families are surrounded by an atmosphere of negative energy. "You're not worth it." "It won't work." "You'll screw it up." "You can't." "You're too stupid." "Life is awful." These are the prevailing beliefs.

4. Negative beliefs. Repeated negative results over many years tend to create negative beliefs that are self-fulfilling prophecies. If you're afraid no one will ever love you, you'll act in ways that make others avoid you, and you'll prove your fear is true. Years of negative energy result in heavily ingrained beliefs about worthlessness, lovelessness, helplessness, and hopelessness. You don't believe life will ever be good, and you don't have the energy to try.

5. Fear, insecurity. The reinforcement of your negative beliefs intensifies the fear that life will never get better and nothing will change. The belief that attempts to change are hopeless and your life will always be miserable is terrifying. It's a repetitive cycle: Learned beliefs and behaviors lead to negative results that reinforce fear and validate old, dysfunctional patterns learned in childhood.

6. Reinforce old habits. Repeating this cycle over and over causes the early beliefs to become more and more ingrained, until they seem indisputable, and leads further around the cycle.

Nick grew up with a mentally disturbed mother, and his experience in childhood led him to believe he was worthless and that nothing would ever go right for him. His despair led him to be depressed, easily discouraged, and irritable. His abrasive nature meant he had trouble getting along with others and had problems at work, including losing several jobs. His wife grew tired of his negative attitude and left him. All of these negative experiences reinforced his beliefs, and he became more and more depressed. This led to a drinking problem, which made everything worse and further reinforced the negative belief system. Nick was caught in a downward spiral.

Making Changes

Being caught in a downward spiral such as Nick's is overwhelming and discouraging. The weight of the ever-increasing negativity, added to the problems brought on by self-destructive behavior, is crushing. People caught in such a trap often believe there is no way out. In fact, one of the fears that fuels the spiral is hopelessness.

But there is a way out. Just as there is a downward, negative spiral, there is also an upward, positive spiral. When a person learns new information that counteracts the early belief system and has support and the courage to act on the new knowledge, things begin to improve, and that provides encouragement and motivation to continue on the new path.

Change is not easy. Not only do you have to fight old habits and beliefs (which often feels as if you're changing who you are), but the people closest to you will often resist the change you are attempting to make. You have to struggle with feeling inept, a new beginner at all sorts of things you used to do automatically. Martin Groder, M.D., author of *Business Games: How to Recognize the Players and Deal with Them,* writes: "Recognize that all change involves loss, even if you're moving to a new neighborhood where life will be more pleasant. You're losing your old way of life, and it's instinctive to want to cling to it—at least to some degree." Even if what you used to do was terribly destructive and led to relationship disasters, career failure, and enormous stress, it was what you knew—and knowing how to change it is not simple or obvious.

Stages of Change

In his book *Changing for Good,* psychology professor James 0. Prochaska, Ph.D., proposes six stage of change:

1. Pre-contemplation

2. Contemplation

3. Preparation

4. Action

5. Maintenance

6. Successful change

Let's explore these stages and how they might apply to changing from dysfunctional habits.

1. **Pre-contemplation.** Before change can be made, we must have an idea of what changes we want. Dr. Prochaska recommends researching the change you're about to make, so you know all the benefits and reasons why the change is desirable. Having a clear idea of the change you want to make, how it will look and feel, and what you will say and do, is a great way to "try the change on" before you actually implement it. The exercises later in this chapter will help you.

2. **Contemplation.** This stage is about getting more deeply into picturing your life after you implement the changes you want to make. What kind of people will you want to have around you? What will you want to do? How will your life look?

3. **Preparation.** In this stage, you break the proposed changes down into small steps that can actually be accomplished. If the steps are detailed and small enough, they seem easier and encourage you to believe you can actually accomplish what you want to do. This is also a good stage for anticipating the support you'll need and where to find it. Do you need new friends? Are there certain members of your family who'll be supportive of your changes? Do you need professional support and guidance? For example, if you decide you need more education to rise above your income level, break the process of getting educated down to the smallest steps possible. 1. Get some school catalogs. 2. Get information about how you can pay for school. 3. Choose a suitable school. 4. Get the help of a counselor at your chosen school to choose a major. And so on.

4. **Action.** Once the steps are in place, the key is to actually do something. This seems obvious, but reluctance to make the first steps is often what stops people from changing. If you have your steps clearly defined, and they are small enough steps to be possible, you may need some encouragement and support to take action. In the example of going back to school, you could find a friend to do it with you, or at least to go with you to get the catalogs and visit the schools.

5. **Maintenance.** Maintaining the energy to keep a change going isn't easy because, after the first exciting new steps, keeping going in your new path gets difficult. All the negative energy of your past will come up to discourage you, and maintaining new behaviors will be difficult at first. The

guidelines and exercises in Chapter 7 will explain the roadblocks to maintaining your new behaviors and what to do about them. For example, you can motivate yourself using celebration and appreciation.

6. **Successful change**. If you follow these steps and maintain the new behaviors for a while, you'll find that it gets easier and easier.

Nick

Nick spent a long time in the *pre-contemplation* and *contemplation* stages, blaming other people and being angry at the world before he ever got into therapy. He thought about therapy and sobriety, read about it, talked to friends about it for several years before he actually decided he wanted to begin to make changes. He *prepared* by visiting a few open Alcoholics Anonymous meetings without making a commitment, just to see what went on. His *action* stage was several years of attending AA meetings and special meetings to study the 12 steps. He also got a sponsor. Once he had a handle on his sobriety, he decided it was time to get into therapy. Working his program, making new friends who were in recovery, and being in therapy gave him the support he needed to *maintain* the changes he was making. After a few years, his life was working well, and he had made a *successful change.*

This works because there is a positive habit-forming cycle that is just as powerful as the negative cycle we discussed earlier. This is illustrated by the following diagram.

New, Functional Habit Cycle

1. **New learning.** Often, the most amazing part of acquiring new, functional habits is learning the difference. As was previously stated, early family experience is so ingrained that it feels like "the way it is"—so finding out that there are other possibilities is both exciting and scary. New possibilities come along when your mind is open to them. Books, workshops, friends, magazines, therapy, and even TV and movies can all be sources of new learning, or at least the initial awareness that different ideas exist. Once you know that something new is possible, following the stages of change will help you implement your new goals.

2. **Thoughtful, new behavior.** Once you've learned new information and decided to change your behavior, you begin to act in new ways, which takes

thought and experimentation. Rather than operating mindlessly, doing things you learned by rote in childhood, you're carefully following the new plan you've laid out. It's tiring, because it takes thinking and effort to overcome what comes "naturally"—the things you learn in childhood. But, if you persist in the new behavior, you'll progress to the next point on the cycle.

3. Positive results. Behaving carefully and consciously produces positive results right away. Suddenly (because you're giving them something different to relate to) people will respond better toward you, and (because your thoughtful actions make more sense) everything you do will be more successful.

4. Positive beliefs. Getting more positive results begins to challenge the old negative beliefs and helps you form new, more positive ways of thinking. After all, if positive things are happening, the old negative ideas are being proven wrong.

5. Confidence. Actual evidence that positive things can happen and that you can be successful and the gradual change of old negative beliefs, all add up to increased confidence. When your life goes better for an extended time, you begin to feel better and trust that you can handle life. Your confidence begins to grow.

6. Reinforce new habits. Each time around, the cycle reinforces you in learning new information and applying it. As your skill at using the new information grows, the positive results increase, and so does your positive belief and confidence, until you're solid in your new belief system.

Sarah

Once Sarah learned to be aware of her leftover anger, she decided to learn new ways of relating to people and letting go of her anger. In therapy, she worked on different ways of relating, allowing people to be who they are, and maintaining her cool. As she began to put this new information into action, her relationships changed. "It seemed like magic to me," Sarah said. "I always thought people didn't like me, I wasn't loveable—that was the way it was. I never connected it to my own behavior. Now, I see that people are responding to me differently, and I can actually change their responses by controlling *myself*. I used to think I had to control the other person. This makes life so much easier, and I now believe I'll find the love I want—and know what to do with it when I do find it."

In this book, we have explored some of the ways family habits and styles can influence us as adults, and how to search for clues to your past. To learn for yourself what Sarah and Nick are discovering, use the following exercise, which will help you release and resolve the triggers and patterns that keep you replicating old, toxic family relationships.

EXERCISE

Releasing and Resolving Patterns and Triggers

This exercise is adapted from the "Time Travel" exercise in my book *The Real 13th Step*. You can use it to explore the early scenes that influence your current relationships. When you find that you are reacting to your mate, your boss, or a relative in old, painful, or emotional ways, you can use this exercise to unearth a memory of emotional, physical, or psychological pain from your childhood that is troubling you. And with minor changes, you can use it for other inner work, too. For example, if you're having a recurring dream that troubles you, you can use this exercise to replay the dream, and the dream won't bother you anymore. By using scenes from the present and the future as well as the past (a quarrel with your current mate, a worrying future encounter with someone who's angry at you, or a presentation you'll be making on Monday), you can use this to detox the situation and practice new skills.

To allow yourself the full impact of the exercise, without interruption, read the following steps into a tape recorder and play them back.

1. Invoke a troubling scene. To begin, sit quietly by yourself, and close your eyes. Visualize yourself as a small child in a scene from childhood that was painful. You will learn how to correct the scene, take care of yourself, and then forgive whoever created the problem, and forgive yourself for your own participation. Allow the troubling scene from your memory to appear around your child self. You may get a mental picture, or, if not, just imagine the scene as you remember it. Remember to use your senses, to establish your scene clearly, unless this is a scene of childhood abuse or incest. In that case, you may find it too painful or stressful to use all the senses, so allow yourself to keep your distance, by just thinking of the scene and not developing as much sensory information. If your scene is very painful, or frightening, view the scene as objectively as you can, as though it is a story about someone else, or a movie.

2. **Enter the scene as an adult.** Like a time traveler from the future, visualize yourself in the scene as the grownup you are today. There will be two of you present, the small child you were and your modern, adult self.

Realizing that the pain of his childhood was at the root of his present anger, Nick went back into his childhood to get release for his anger. He pictured himself going back into his childhood home, the scene of the terrible abuse and neglect he suffered as a child.

3. **Take charge of the scene.** Now it's time to take charge of the scene and protect your child self. Do whatever is needed to stop the adults or other children from upsetting, hurting, or neglecting your child self. If the other children or adults are too badly behaved, you can make them leave or remove your child self— if you want to. You have total power here, in your imagination. Use that power to make a safe environment and to provide protection for your child self. If you like, you can also surround your child self with loving people.

Nick took some time to befriend his child-self He took charge, and made sure that he prevented any harm from coming to his child self

4. **Take care of your child.** As the child in this scene, you may feel frightened, angry, confused, feeling helpless, or overwhelmed with grief. As the adult, you should be rational, effective, competent, and reassuring. You may encounter some resistance to doing this, in the form of feeling incapable of taking care of your child self. But remember: You can do this over and over in your mind until you get it right. You can try to fix the situation in several different ways, before you decide which is best.

Visualize removing your child self from danger; comfort and reassure; correct any lies your child self was told (that he was stupid, or it was her fault) by telling your child the (positive) truth (he is intelligent, no child causes her own abuse); and take time to begin to establish a friendship with your child self. If you see that your child self needs some information or help, provide it. Promise that your child will never be left at the mercy of ignorant, malicious, incompetent, or uncomprehending people again.

Once the child in the scene trusted him, he took him out of the house and away from the traumatic events. Nick assured his child self "You're safe now, and I'm going to make sure you stay safe."

5. When your child self feels *safe*, discuss forgiveness. When you have corrected the scene enough that your child is out of danger and feeling safe, talk with your child about what happened. Discuss what went wrong and who made mistakes, and decide how to avoid being the victim of those same mistakes again. Once you and your child both know he or she will not be hurt again (because you'll do what it takes to protect him or her), you'll find that your child will be ready to forgive the people who hurt him or her and will understand that they just don't know how to behave. Help your child see that whatever happened was not his or her fault, and your child self doesn't have to make the same mistakes the others made or repeat the mistakes he or she made.

Nick and little Nicky talked about what had happened, how sick Nick's schizophrenic and alcoholic mother was. Nick realized that his father was overwhelmed and didn't know what to do about his Jive children and crazy wife, so he just hid out at work and let the children fend for themselves. Nick knew his parents had been wrong to treat him as they did, but he also understood that it was their ignorance and fear, not himself that caused them to mistreat him. Although he couldn't forgive them, he began to understand why he always felt so hopeless, helpless, and enraged. Nick pictured his adult self-soothing and comforting his child self.

6. **Take your child to a safe place.** Close the scene by visualizing your child self in a safe, secure place, completely out of danger. Reassure him or her that you'll be there when you're needed, and tell him or her how to get your attention when he or she feels in danger. This means that your adult, rational self will not leave your emotional, child self alone, dependent, and at the mercy of people who are hurtful. Do not leave the scene until your child self feels calm and secure.

After their discussion, Nick imagined taking little Nicky to Nick's present home. He made a special place for him by putting his childhood picture and some childhood toys in a special place. Nick assured his child self that he was safe now and that Nick would make sure he stayed safe. He imagined hugging Nicky and said Nicky could call him whenever he needed him for protection.

7. Repeat regularly. After you have done this exercise the first time, you can keep your promise to keep your child self-safe (and build self-trust) by time-traveling back to your child self as often as needed, until it becomes an unconscious habit. Once you've done this many times and become proficient, you will not need to close your eyes to be in instant contact with your child self; you will be able to imagine being with your child self at any time. Doing this exercise repeatedly, whenever things go wrong and bring up old, painful memories, will eventually clear out your childhood traumas and correct the damage done in childhood, while helping you build new patterns of behavior and reinforce positive beliefs. You'll find that you instinctively know when someone or something is hurtful to you and when you're being hurtful to others. You'll also know what to do to correct the situation (don't be alone with violent or emotionally hurtful people, don't allow yourself to be in tempting situations, and so on), and you'll feel safe enough to forgive those who are confused and behave in hurtful ways, because their behavior will not be dangerous to you.

With practice, and by going back to other scenes where Nicky was upset and keeping him safe, Nick found that he was much more comfortable with people. He began to let go of his fear and anger, the knot of tension in his stomach began to relax, and he started to relate more comfortably to other people. Nick found that he saw other people differently, too. He could keep his distance from people who didn't treat others well, and he could easily recognize the people who were safe and healthy for him.

By learning how to use these tools, and then applying them to your specific issues, you can move from old, negative dysfunctional behaviors to new, thoughtful, and positive ones. With new information and habits, you can build a new conception of self, freed from the old definitions and beliefs. Once you're in charge of your own behavior, you can resolve old problems and free yourself to run your own life.

Chapter 7. Removing Roadblocks to Creating Your Future

Man is most uniquely human when he turns obstacles into opportunities.
—**Eric Hoffer**

The skills you've learned already: understanding how and what you learned in childhood, identifying how you react to people who remind you of family members, identifying how your beliefs and habits were acquired, and learning how to change your old patterns and beliefs will take some time— but with persistence, you can change a lot in a few months. Once you understand how your reactions and responses to life and to people are programmed by your past, you can change the programming, which means you can get in charge of your own life.

Once you've rejected the grip your past has on you, and you're in control, you need to decide what kind of life you want to create for yourself. Without those old negative beliefs and habits to hold you back, you can improve your life today and plan to create the future you never even dared to dream of. You can improve your relationships, your financial situation, your social life, and your home life.

Roadblocks on Your Path

Coming from a dysfunctional early family, however, might have created some roadblocks on your new path. Some of the most common internal roadblocks are lack of motivation, worry, failure to plan, emotional blockages, and relationship problems. In this chapter, you'll learn how to remove all these roadblocks and learn more positive habits to replace them.

Lack of Motivation

Self-motivation is the ability to mobilize your own energy in service of getting what you want. If you know how to create your own energy, you can keep yourself going through the process of creating what you want.

Lack of motivation is a roadblock, because it drains your energy and keeps you from reaching your goals. Perhaps you are not motivated enough on the job, not able to keep your resolution to diet, get work done, quit smoking, or follow through on your goals and decisions. To succeed, you need to know how to create both positive and negative motivation—to be energized enough to accomplish things or to stop undesirable behaviors.

Most people have tried unsuccessfully to pressure themselves into changing with negative internal messages, such as, "If you don't exercise you'll be fat," or "If you don't work all weekend you'll mess up the presentation," or "You'll die of cancer because you're smoking." At times, you probably have tried bribing or persuading yourself, which works for a while, but eventually fails. Alternatively, you may have gotten another person to coerce you, such as a motivational group, hypnosis, a parent or parent substitute, who will insist that you have to behave.

This last option may work quite well for some time. But if you repeatedly criticize yourself or get someone else to apply pressure, you'll quickly feel oppressed and rebellious. Intimidation and pressure eventually leads to paralysis and procrastination.

Creating Motivation

As I explained previously in this book, the only kind of motivation that works permanently grows out of celebration and appreciation. It's easy to remember in equation form:

CELEBRATION + APPRECIATION = MOTIVATION

When you find a way to appreciate yourself for what you've already accomplished, and to celebrate your previous successes, you will find you are naturally motivated to accomplish more. No struggle, no hassle—you accomplish out of the pure joy of success! In my lectures and workshops, I use the concept of two possible employers to illustrate this: the "bad boss" and the "good boss."

The **Bad** Boss

> ➤ Operates through intimidation and criticism.

> ➤ Always complains; never praises (silence means you're doing OK).

➢ Gets nasty if you make a mistake.

➢ Humiliates you in front of others.

➢ Never thinks you've done enough.

➢ Assumes you are lazy and dishonest.

➢ Changes the rules arbitrarily.

➢ Is never satisfied or pleased.

The **Good** Boss

➢ Praises frequently.

➢ Always lets you know when you're doing well.

➢ Asks you what you need whenever you've made a mistake.

➢ Is very helpful.

➢ Is concerned about your well-being as well as your productivity.

➢ Assumes you want to do a good job.

➢ Helps you feel like part of the team.

➢ Treats you as a valued human being.

➢ Is clear about the duties expected of you.

Both of these bosses have the same goal: to get the job done, but there is a big difference in the success of their individual management styles.

What would your reaction be to working with each of these bosses? If you worked for the bad boss, you would probably work in an atmosphere of tension and anger. You'd work only to keep the boss off your back and would be tempted to goof off whenever he or she is not around. You would not be at your most efficient, because you'd be stressed and resentful.

If you were working for this boss, how would you feel? Would you go to work happily each day? Would you volunteer for extra work? Would you look forward to each new assignment? Probably not. In short, you would not feel highly motivated, would you?

On the other hand, working for the good boss would tend to make you care about your productivity and your job. You'd take pride in your accomplishments and be eager to learn more and accomplish more. Even in such a boss's absence, you would work well, be motivated, and feel gratified and appreciated. Anything your boss asks will be met with a cooperative response.

How would you feel? Would you feel eager to please this boss? Would you look forward to his or her reaction to your latest work? Would you be willing to help out if extra work were necessary? Most likely, you would. You would feel enthusiastic and motivated, and look forward to work each day.

Which boss would you rather work for?

Your Internal Boss

In your own life you have a choice about how to manage yourself. If you choose to be a good boss to yourself, you'll be kind, understanding, very generous with praise, and gentle with corrections. You'll learn to use the two "magic motivators": celebration and appreciation.

As a result, you'll accomplish your goals with a sense of pride and achievement and a great deal of pleasure. You will feel motivated and wonder why you never realized how easy it was.

Motivating Yourself with Appreciation

Most of us know how to appreciate others. However, we feel embarrassed and uncomfortable if we are too generous with self-praise. Dysfunctional families often told us not to brag or to be cocky when we were young, and self-appreciation comes awkwardly. However, if you want to create motivation, knowing how to use self-appreciation becomes necessary and desirable too. The good news is that you can learn it.

Guidelines for learning self-appreciation

To become proficient in self-appreciation, try the following:

> **Make a note.** Write positive comments on your daily calendar to yourself for jobs well done or any achievements you want to celebrate. Or you can paste stickers on your daily calendar as you accomplish goals daily. Frequent positive commentary is a very effective way to reward yourself and remind yourself of your success.

> **Look to your childhood.** Use activities that felt like a celebration in your childhood: Did your family toast a celebration with champagne or sparkling cider, a gathering of friends, or a thankful prayer? Create a celebration environment: Use balloons, music, flowers, or candles, or set your table with the best china. Use the exercise on your family style in Chapter 2 to find ideas.

> **Use visible reminders.** Surround yourself with visible evidence of your successes. Plant a commemorative rosebush or get a new houseplant to mark a job well done, or display photos of fun events and sports or hobby trophies. It's a constant reminder that you appreciate yourself, and when you see them daily you'll feel the appreciation.

> ➤ **Reward yourself.** The latest best-seller you've been dying to read can be a great reward/celebration for reading your required technical books.

> ➤ **Party.** Celebrate a cherished friendship with an impromptu lunchtime picnic and a balloon or with tickets to a ball game.

By celebrating your accomplishments, however small, you will create motivation to accomplish more. Get creative with your celebrations. Above all, have fun.

Maintain Control of Your Life

If you find yourself around someone who takes command and tells you what you should be doing or offers unsolicited comments about how you are doing things wrong or otherwise appoints him- or herself as the boss in your life, you may find your newly created motivation flagging. A memory of some old directive or belief you got from a family member may get in the way. Remember: You can mentally fire anyone who tries to be your (internal) boss—of course, I'm not talking about the person who pays your salary. This is about your personal life decisions. It's your life, and you are in charge of what plan you file. Anytime you have to "fire" a bad boss, you may need to remind yourself of how much you have accomplished without that kind of help. Celebrate your independence, your spirit, your willingness to be responsible for yourself.

It is also possible to set up informative books, articles, television authorities, gurus, and the like as your boss—in which case you again will find your rebellion rising and your motivation flagging. These informational aids can be useful, but only if your keep them in perspective.
A good boss gets information about how to run things, gets educated, goes for help when necessary, but remains in charge. Information is there for your use, but no outside expert can know what is right for you. As your own internal boss, you can sort through the facts wisely and judiciously, reject what does not suit your style, personality, or goals, and use the rest to further and celebrate your accomplishments.

Whenever you find your motivation flagging, look around for how you are doing at being your boss. Are you using a motivational, supportive style? Have you let someone else take over your internal authority? Is there some appreciation you need?

Take a few minutes with yourself every day just for appreciation. It's easy, fun, and very effective. Imagine living every day energized and motivated!

Once you've learned to keep yourself motivated, encouraged, and supported with your "inner good boss," you may still find that you still have a problem with worrying about the future—things that could happen or that haven't been done properly. Such worry is a roadblock that can really stop you in your tracks.

Worry

Worry is obsessive thinking about possible problems, things you forgot to do, things you might do wrong, things that might happen, what other people might do or not do. Worry drains your energy, keeps you from thinking clearly, and causes anxiety, hopelessness, and helplessness. Removing the roadblock of worry will help you to stay on track and keep your energy high.

You can transform your worry into confidence and eagerness. If your early family history was full of unexpected catastrophes, unplanned hassles, and people who were racked with anxiety and worry, it's more constructive to replace your worry with anticipation.

Anticipation involves thinking through the possibilities and planning for the unexpected as well as the expected events and circumstances, but if your thoughts turn negative your anticipation can become worry. If you think about the bad things that could happen, without figuring out what you can do about it, you'll just go around and around, getting more and more anxious: "What if my car breaks down?" "What if I don't get the job?" and so on. The way to avoid this is to treat the questions as genuine, and answer them: "If my car breaks down, I'll borrow some money and get it repaired." Or, "If I don't get this job, I'll keep searching until I find one."

Negative worrying can be turned into positive anticipation when it leads you to consider alternate possibilities and plan for future events. If your anxiety level is so high that just answering your own questions doesn't work, or if you worry a lot, have anxiety attacks, or dread making decisions and being in charge, use the following steps to help you turn your free-flowing anxiety into focused anticipation. Here are the guidelines I give my clients for handling worry.

The Worrier's Guidelines

If you worry a lot, can't sleep, have anxiety attacks, or obsessively think about future events and problems when you should be concentrating on other things, following these simple steps will help you transform your worry into action:

1. **Write it down.** If you're feeling anxious or worried or you can't stop thinking about some future event, take a few moments to write down whatever is worrying you. If you can't write it down, think it through carefully until you can clearly say what you're worrying about. Clarifying your worries will stop the free-floating sensation of anxiety with no basis.

2. **Evaluate.** Think about the first item on your list. Ask yourself, "Is there anything I can do about it now?" If you're at home and worrying about the office, or if the problem won't occur until next week or next year, you may not be able to do anything about it right now. Or you may be worrying about a problem you can do something about, such as calling someone, getting an estimate of costs, or making a doctor's appointment to check out a worrisome symptom.

3. **Do something. If** there is something you can do, do it. Sometimes, worry is a way to procrastinate. Often, worry is a way to keep a mental list going, as in "I'm worried that I'll forget to bring the slides for the presentation tomorrow."

   ➢ If you're worrying about how your presentation will go at work tomorrow, go over your notes and lay out your clothes for the morning.

   ➢ If you're worried about a health problem, look up the illness or injury on the internet, or call your doctor and ask some questions.

   ➢ If you're at work worrying about cooking dinner when you get home, write down a menu or a list of ingredients.

   ➢ If you're worried that you may be fired, update your resume and call some agencies. You don't have to take another job, but if there's a real problem you'll be prepared.

Here's an example: If you're worried that the roof may leak the next time it rains, start making a list about what you can do about it. Your inner dialogue may sound like this:

"The weather report calls for rain next week. I'm worried that the roof might leak."

"Call a roofing company and have them look at it."

"I'm worried that a roofing company will charge me more than they should because I don't know how much it should cost."

"Call my brother (or my neighbor, or my friend) who had his roof done, and ask him what it cost, and also if he liked the contractor he used."

"Okay."

When you reach this "okay," it's time to make the call, or if it's too late at night, make a note to call the next day.

4. **Distract yourself.** When you've done what you can, or made your lists or notes, then distract yourself. Get busy doing something else: Read, take a walk, or take a bath. If the worrisome thoughts arise, remind yourself that you've done everything you can do, and bring your focus back to what you're doing now.

If you consistently repeat these steps every time you find yourself worrying, you'll learn to think more constructively, and, over time, you'll feel more confident and positive. You can use the energy you save in not worrying to achieve the more positive attitudes of anticipation.

Failure to Plan

One of the biggest roadblocks to creating the life you want is failure to plan. The hopelessness learned in a dysfunctional childhood can make it seem useless and unnecessary to have plans and dreams. When you overcome those old beliefs and allow yourself to have positive thoughts about your future, you can replace worry with anticipation. When you approach life with anticipation instead of worry, your energy rises, and life seems a lot easier. To establish a habit of daily anticipation, use the following method.

Daily Anticipation: Either in the evening or the morning, take 15 to 20 minutes to sit down with your calendar and think about the day to come. Consider your to-do list, your appointments (whatever kind of appointments you have: with a business associate, a customer, your dentist, to take your child to soccer or ballet, or lunch with a friend), and whatever you personally would like to accomplish

> (for example: gardening, cooking dinner, making a speech, writing your novel, working out, winning at a sport, meditating or praying, creating art or music, or visiting a friend).

If your list is more than you can possibly get done in one day, sort through it now, instead of waiting until the end of the day to find you didn't accomplish the most important things. Prioritize what you have to do, and whatever you're not going to get to today, put on your to-do list for tomorrow or next week.

Look at your calendar and schedule as realistically as you can. For example, if you are taking your daughter to ballet class or your son to football practice, consider that it might be important to allow enough time for the two of you to talk. If the client you have to see is long-winded or habitually late, take that into consideration. If you are extra tired, consider not packing your day as full as usual.

On the other hand, if your calendar is not full enough, if you have a tendency to go to work and then come home with no idea of what you'll do for the evening, then give some thought to scheduling some of that unused time. For example, volunteer to help somewhere, invite a friend to dinner, participate in a sport, join the church choir, or take a class.

In this way you can take charge of your day, and make sure that, within the limits of your real situation, you do the things that are most important to you. The few minutes you take at the beginning of your day to organize it can save you hours later. If you focus on planning each day, you will make steady progress toward attaining your future goals.

Emotional Blockages

Emotions are natural occurrences, common responses to people and events. When kept in proper perspective, they enhance your experience of life and help you deal with problems. Properly used, emotions are part of the healing process. But when they are blocked or overactive and out of control, they can become roadblocks. Inappropriate emotional reactions create drama and confusion where it is not necessary and can sidetrack you from getting your life to be what you want. I use the following metaphor with my clients to help them understand the proper relationship of emotions: Emotions represent the amazing ability of our bodies to express and relate to the dramatic, tender, fearsome, and sentimental aspects of life.

Emotions as Weather

Emotions (tears, panic attacks, angry outbursts, withdrawal, depression, elation, lust, romantic excitement, euphoria) are the weather conditions of the inner self.

Being afraid of, ashamed of, or embarrassed by your feelings is akin to being afraid of the weather. Certainly there are weather conditions that are fearsome, such as hurricanes, earthquakes, floods, exploding volcanoes, and fierce fires, and we need to control these if we can, and protect ourselves from them. But most emotional climate conditions are pretty mild.

My clients have found it very helpful to use the metaphors of weather to understand how natural and normal *all* feelings are. Here are my thoughts on the basics of emotional weather. It's a concept I'm just working out, so please share your ideas and reactions.

Sunshine

Your smile lights up your face the way the sun lights our day. Smiles, too, can come from behind clouds or after emotional storms. The smile signals that all is well, pressure is equalized, and the coast is clear to be out and open and have some fun.

Rain

As can rain, tears can be stormy or just a light sprinkle, feel angry, cold, dreary, and sad, or even come through the sunshine. Rain often follows a change of weather pressure, and tears can be the result of a release of inner tension. People frequently cry from relief that they've been heard or that they can see a solution where there appeared to be a problem. Those who suffer from a trauma or a loss normally cry a little *after* the first shock of finding out, as the awful pressure of the news is absorbed and the grief sets in.

Rain first carries with it the dust suspended in the air, and then washes everything clean as it continues. Emotional rain, too, can first be painful and then begin to bring release and clarity. A "good cry" is one that really lets go of the held feelings and continues until relief sets in.

Rainbows

When you allow the tears to flow until your natural smile returns, you will feel hopeful again. Hope is the rainbow of our internal climate. As is the case with a rainbow, hope doesn't exist until there has been a disappointment and the disappointment has been accepted completely enough to let the sun shine once more. That smile, coming thorough sadness, brings with it a renewed feeling of hope.

Storms

Sometimes reluctance to express unhappiness or discomfort builds pressure that eventually releases in a rush. Violent storms shake things up, just as strong anger does. Anger that is allowed to get out of control is as destructive as a hurricane, but anger that is expressed in healthy ways can "clear the air" just as a storm does. The aftermath of a *healthy,* not-too-violent storm allows us to appreciate the pleasures of calmness.

Cloudiness and fog

Emotionally, things are not always very clear. It's normal to feel foggy and unsure or depressed and dark from time to time. If you can remember it's just your emotional climate, and explore it to discover the cause, the fog will lift, the clouds will part, it may rain or storm a little, but the sun will eventually come out again. Normal depression that is not allowed to take its natural course, not opened up to let the fresh air in, can turn into emotional smog or internal pollution.

Smog

Emotional smog, akin to the weather smog, is just the normal cloudy/foggy conditions with manmade junk added. We call it clinical depression. Everyone is down from time to time, but those who attack themselves when down, or have others around who pollute their internal atmosphere with criticism or shaming, become smog-bound and can't clear up their internal atmosphere. Letting in the fresh air of interest and the warmth of emotional support allows the fog to lift and the sun to come out again.

Internal conditions

If you try to pay the same amount of daily attention to your internal conditions as you probably do to the weather report and begin to regard your feelings as naturally as weather, you'll become much more emotionally comfortable. As is the weather, your feelings are easier to accept and live with when you manage them, respond to them, and don't try to resist them or deny them, If you understand your feelings as weather, you can have many lovely inner days.

Your Sense of Emotion

Human attributes, we are taught, include five senses: sight, sound, taste, touch, and smell. Only in science fiction do we read about a sixth sense, which is usually depicted as a psychic sense. If you think about it, however, your emotions are your real "sixth sense." Just as your other five senses do, your emotions register data about the external world. With your sight, your eyes take in data about colors, shapes, and relative sizes of the things in the world around us. Touch tells us how things feel, how warm, cold, soft, hard, sharp, or smooth they are.

Your emotions tell you what others' feelings are. We can sense, in an almost psychic way, how someone feels at a distance, without being told. By comparing what our other senses tell us about others (smiles, frowns, tension, "prickly vibes," relaxed breathing, and an indescribable type of data we call *empathy)* with what we know about our own inner feelings, we draw conclusions about what other people are feeling. Without being told, we know when someone is angry, when someone has strong positive or negative feelings toward us, and when we are loved.

With conscientious practice, people can improve their use of senses, such as being a wine taster, reading Braille, refining your sense of color as an artist, or learning to tell different fabrics by texture. Certain people, such as psychotherapists and actors, practice and refine emotions until they can sense very small changes. As a psychotherapist, I "read" my clients' emotions and give them feedback to help them sort out emotional confusion. "You say you're fine, but you appear to be angry," I might say to someone who is disconnected from his feelings.

Sight is an external sense—we only see what's outside us. Touch, however, is both internal and external. We can feel food go down our gullet, on occasion we can feel our own heartbeat, and we can feel muscle cramps and movement from inside the body. Emotions are a sense that is simultaneously internal and external. To our emotions, it's as if there's no limit to our bodies, and our skin is transparent. We feel our feelings on the inside, and yet they reach out and touch people and tell us what they're feeling, too. It is a type of psychic sense, especially to people who develop it.

Just as your sight helps you navigate the roads, avoid obstacles, and choose the best route, your emotions are the sense that help you navigate the paths of relationships. If you are knowledgeable about your feelings, and your sensitivity to others' feelings, you can be much more effective in all your relationships, maximizing your love, your intimacy, your emotional well-being, and your happiness.

Practicing Emotion

You can refine and sensitize yourself to your feelings by "tracking" what you are feeling on a daily basis: Just stop a few times each day and ask yourself, "What am I feeling right now?" Once you get comfortable with that, you can spend some time people-watching and guess what they might be feeling. You won't know if you've guessed right unless you ask, but just practicing paying attention will sharpen your skills.

Relationship Problems

Most people would agree that relationship problems can be life's major roadblock. An intimate relationship that is stressful, painful, and upsetting consumes enormous amounts of energy. Volatile relationships with family members are also draining. Even problems with people at work or with neighbors can be distressing. Growing up in a dysfunctional family can leave you short of skills for improving relationships. The following techniques—communication basics, state of the union meetings, and the relationship reservoir—will give you the basics to help you improve all your relationships.

We'll begin with improving communication, because it's the most basic and frequently used relationship skill.

Guidelines for Improving Communication

1. Seek first to understand. If you know your partner's frame of reference, you can speak to him or her within it.

2. Pay attention to how your words are landing. If your companion's response looks off the mark for what you said, check out what he or she is hearing: Ask your companion what he or she heard you say.

3. Focus on the solution that would work for everyone, rather than who's right or wrong. Only focus on the problem long enough to understand, then switch to what will fix it.

4. Separate emotion from solution. If one or both of you are upset, irrational, or reactive, you aren't communicating. Take a break and try again in a few minutes, when both of you have calmed down.

5. Don't beat dead horses. If you've been over the same ground several times with no forward movement, get some help. An objective third party can work wonders.

6. Be nice. Strive to create a cooperative atmosphere, and consider your partner's feelings.

If you approach all your important communications with these guidelines in mind, you'll find that your interactions with people improve, and you'll have the first step toward improving understanding.

Once you have established an effective method of communicating, if you make sure you create the opportunity at regular intervals, you'll keep your communication up to date and timely.

State of the Union Meetings

Whether you are single, dating or married or have a family of your own, making sure you have a regular weekly meeting date to discuss the state of the relationship will make a tremendous difference in the emotional tenor of the relationship. When you have a regular chance to talk about what's going on in the relationship, then problems, resentment, and frustration don't get a chance to build. If you have children, every member of your family has a right to have his or her opinions respected. You don't have to agree or go along with what your child or spouse wants, but you should at least know what it is, and your child should know why you're overriding his or her preferences. Regular couple or family meetings, where everyone including the children expresses feelings, negative and positive, and all of you work together to solve problems, can help a lot.

Begin couple or family meetings as early in the relationship as possible, whether you think you have any issues to discuss or not. If you set a pattern of doing this early in a relationship, it will be easy to expand the group to include children if you have them. For relationships and families that are already established, it might feel a bit awkward to begin the meetings at first, but if you follow the steps that follow, everyone will soon experience the value of having an appropriate time and place to talk about issues and plans.

Sit down on a weekly basis with your partner or family, and discuss everything about your relationship, positive and problematic, and how it's going for each of you. If you have small children, include them and get their input, also. Choose a time when everyone can get together weekly, and suggest to everyone that you order pizza or cook something they like.

Begin the session with a brief prayer or blessing and a round of complements, where each member gives a complement to every other member. This creates a positive atmosphere.

At the meeting, everyone (including you) can follow these steps:

1. **Gratitude.** Each person states a positive thing about each person in the family, preferably something that has happened this week. For example, "I really appreciate how much you helped me this week when you knew I had a deadline at work." Or, "I noticed that you made a big effort to keep the kitchen clean." Or, "Thank you for your sense of humor. It really helps when you make me laugh when I'm getting too serious." Be sure to thank the person after praising them. If you follow a religious tradition, you can open the meeting by giving thanks in the manner of your faith.

2. **Improvements.** Each person then mentions one thing they want to improve and what they want to do to make it better. Small children will need help until they understand, but they will catch on quickly. Even you and one child can do this. The rule is that, in order to bring up a complaint, you must have a suggestion for a solution, even if you don't think it's the best possible solution.

3. **Problem-solving.** If anyone has a problem to solve, he or she can describe it, and then ask for help from the group to solve it. Everyone can work together to come up with a solution. Be careful not to allow the description of the problem to deteriorate into criticism and complaining. To state a problem use matter-of-fact terms, and use *I messages:* "I get discouraged and frustrated when the house gets messy." "We need to come up with some money to fix the car." "I have a problem at school." "I need help figuring out how not to fight with Susie anymore."

This simple meeting will do more for the state of your intimate or family relationship than you can imagine. If you deal with them early and approach them with a team spirit of solving them together, most problems can be solved before they become disasters.

Your Relationship Reservoir

Every relationship (including those with family, with friends, and between parents and children) has what I call the "relationship reservoir." Over the course of your relationship, the interaction between you—every kind or unkind word, every gesture of support or criticism, every honest or dishonest interaction between you, every gesture of affection or coldness, add up over the time you spend together.

If you fill your reservoir with good feelings, forgiveness, support, honesty, appreciation, caring, affection, emotional intimacy (and sexual intimacy where appropriate), you build up a backlog of good will and affection—your memories will be warm and mutually admiring.

If you fill it with coldness, criticism, ingratitude, dishonesty, demands, and dissatisfaction, you'll have a reservoir of resentment and disdain.

Each time your relationship makes demands on you as a result of major problems, separations, disagreements, illnesses, and stress, you will draw on your relationship reservoir. If you have built up a supply of good feelings and goodwill with your daily interaction, you'll cheerfully give what's asked of you. If not, whatever's asked will seem like too much to give.

The skills you've learned in this chapter will help you to make a success out of your life. Now all you need is a plan for success, which you'll formulate in the next chapter.

Chapter 8 The Successful Life

Self-trust is the first secret of success.
—Ralph Waldo Emerson

By using the exercises and information in the previous chapters, you have learned where your habits, beliefs, and problems originated, and you have practiced new skills, established new habits and beliefs, and learned tools you can use to create a life that really feels like yours. Now, all you need is a goal and a direction, a plan for building the successful life you want.

Knowing What You Want

It's easy to say you need a goal and a direction, but it takes more than words to actually accomplish it. Choosing the right direction requires knowing what you want and what will feel successful to you. The following exercises will help you to focus on your life and your future and make successful choices.

The next exercise will help you build on the self-awareness skills you already have acquired, and stimulate your individual thinking.

EXERCISE

Consulting Yourself

Many people go through their lives asking everyone else's opinion but never getting clear on their own viewpoint. Others are spending a lot of money these days going to "life coaches." As a therapist, I have always done a certain amount of coaching, giving my clients information and advice and helping them make better life and career choices. But my goal is always to help clients become their own life coaches. These are the steps I ask them to follow:

Steps to Being Your Own Life Coach

1. **Ask your own opinion.** At frequent intervals (about five times a day) during your regular workday, ask yourself:
"What do *I* think about this? Do I like it? Does it make sense to me? Do I agree or disagree with the others? If I had unlimited power, what would I do?" By doing this, you'll get used to asking *your own opinion* of ideas and events.

2. **Listen to the answer.** Listen to your opinions as you would to the ideas of a respected friend. Consider them, weigh them, and even discuss them with yourself from time to time. Allow them to influence your daily thought. If you feel, for example, that your work is not satisfying enough, just accept and allow that feeling to be there, and it will eventually create a need to act and many exciting ideas for how to act. There is no need to act on your ideas yet; just practice listening to your own opinion for now.

3. **Repeat to make decision-making easier**. After you practice asking your own opinion faithfully for a few weeks, it will become automatic to have personal opinions about everything around you. If you don't pressure yourself, but let your ideas incubate at their own pace, this awareness of your own opinion will have a profound effect on what you do and how you act. Activating your individual thinking ability will gradually increase your options and choices and make decision-making faster and easier.

Once you get used to consulting your own opinion on whatever choices you're facing, you will feel much more secure in making decisions.

No one knows what the future will bring. All we can do is evaluate the options and make an informed guess about what results our choices will bring. To help my clients evaluate options, I teach them how to look ahead for possible consequences and outcomes. A chess master is an expert because he can look at the chessboard, work out every possible move that might be made, and then consider all the possible consequences. No matter what move his opponent makes, a master chess player will have already foreseen the move and has an idea of what he wants to do in response. You can use similar techniques to help you make the best possible decisions about your future.

EXERCISE

Future Projection

1. Picture your future. Spend time imagining the future you'd like to happen. If everything in your life went as well as possible, where will you be five years from now? What will your home life be like? What about your work or career? What kind of social life will you have? Use your senses, including feelings, to make the picture as real as possible. What colors are in the scenes? What sounds? What is the temperature like? What are you feeling? What are others feeling? Take as much time as you need to visualize your future as completely as possible. You can visit this imaginary future several times over several days if you like. *For example, perhaps you'd like to be a teacher.*

2. Picture your path. What would you need to do now to make this future happen in five years? Without considering whether you think it's possible, or whether you're willing, figure out what steps you'd need to take to realize your fantasy future. If you need to write down each aspect of your life, and break each aspect down into steps on paper, do so. *In the teaching example, you can decide that you need more education than you have, a teaching credential, and so on.*

3. Make some choices. If any of the beginning steps toward creating your future reality seem desirable, choose some things you actually want to do— even if you aren't sure you know what to do or how to do it. The next step will help with that problem. *Perhaps you aren't absolutely sure you want to teach, but you can choose to get more education, or tutor teenagers, or do something else that's related to teaching to see how it feels.*

4. **Do research.** Look for realistic information to help you figure out what steps you actually need to take. Find people who are doing what you want to do, read biographies, first-person accounts, and descriptions of it, ask questions of people who are involved, and watch movies or plays about the subject. *For example, it is possible to interview teachers of all kinds. Perhaps there even someone in your family who teaches, or a teacher from your past experience. Auditing classes is also possible. You can read teacher novels, histories, and biographies and watch fictional depictions of teachers either in the movies or on TV to give yourself more information.*

5. **Allow the fantasy time to develop into reality.** All new ventures must begin with imagination or fantasy, because there is no real experience to draw on. A wonderful fantasy energizes you to actualize it and bring it into reality. But the process of creating a reality based on the dream changes the dream. As you learn the requirements of achieving real results, you'll find your idea of how your future should look gradually maturing and becoming more realistic. *In our teaching example, you can have a fantasy of being a tenured professor at an Ivy League college, but as you go through the education and training you find that working in an inner-city school helping needy children has a lot more meaning for you (or vice-versa).*

Although some people can tell you their dreams the minute you ask, others have to struggle to figure it out. If you have trouble coming up with a vision of your future that feels satisfying, the following section will help you create motivation, a sense of meaning, and a purpose.

Purpose and Power

"Whatever your age," writes Dr. Bernie Siegel in *Peace, Love and Healing,* "if you learn to listen, your inner voice will speak to you about your path...your 'job on earth'. This wisdom that is directing you from within is your birthright... an inner message, an inner awareness that says, 'This is your path, this is how you can be the best human being possible.' If you follow it, you will achieve your full growth and full potential as a human being....."

Catalysts: Internal and External

When you are in touch with your own inner wisdom, you have a way to choose what is right for you and what is not. But getting in touch with that inner direction takes a catalyst of some kind—a motivator to get us to look for meaning. Sometimes the catalyst is external. For example, the same overwhelming issues that can be discouraging in the news and media (racial and other prejudice; addiction and self-destruction; political oppression in its many forms—starvation, war, torture, misinformation, imprisonment, denial of rights of speech, health and human dignity, and just plain bigotry and nastiness) can also be motivating, if you choose one aspect and make it your cause or your reason. Often the catalyst is internal—a sense of meaning that grows out of spiritual or personal values, the turmoil from a dysfunctional childhood, or even inner pain, and which begins the adventure of finding your "job on earth." Did you know that problems with compulsive eating, substance abuse, destructive addictive relationships, and obsessive behavior are most often misguided attempts to satisfy the heart's desire?

Humans are such amazing miracles of creation. In my practice, I have seen over and over that within each person is a driving force that will not give up and go away. You can attempt to avoid it:

➤ To drown it out with loud, raucous living.

➤ To anesthetize it with food, drink, or drugs.

➤ To avoid it through some obsession or compulsion.

➤ To ignore it by working obsessively.

➤ To be too overwhelmed with drama and agony to notice it.

But as soon as the unavoidable quiet moment happens, there it is, urging them on. Often, people misread this uncomfortable inner restlessness and call it "fear" or "loneliness," but it is only the call of the heart. Until you acknowledge it, it will not allow you to be at peace. Believe it or not, your heart, like everyone's, is filled with purpose and meaning and will constantly press you to discover your true desire and act upon it.

I find that many people who come to me for counseling are *autophobic*— *afraid* of themselves. They are afraid of feeling their own emotions, afraid of being forced to be alone with themselves, afraid to find out what is actually inside them. This irrational fear actually comes down to fearing the power within. We can run very fast and create a lot of damage in an attempt to escape who we are. But the only thing required to find your inner purpose is the courage to be you—to face your fears, to believe in yourself, to be willing to follow your dreams.

A riddle written by philosopher and writer P.L. Travers captures the mystery of the search for inner meaning: "I give you something, you know not what, enrich it, you know not how, bring it back, you know not when. And remember, I shall be watching you.' Said the Sun to the newborn child"

Organizational psychologist and educator Marsha Sinetar describes the risk: "To find in ourselves what makes life worth living is risky business," she writes in *Ordinary People as Monks and Mystics,* "for it means that once we know it we must seek it. It also means that without it life will be valueless."

Famed philosopher Joseph Campbell, on the other hand, warned of the consequences of *not* searching for meaning:

> "If the person insists on a certain program, and doesn't listen to the demands of his own heart, he's going to risk a schizophrenic crackup," he wrote in *Myth and the Quest for Meaning.* "Such a person has put himself off center. He has aligned himself with a program for life, and it's not the one the body's interested in at all. The world is full of people who have stopped listening to themselves or have listened only to their neighbors to learn what they ought to do, how they ought to behave, and what the values are that they should be living for.. .my analysis of the human situation is that we would rather *feel* alive than *be* alive. Sometimes it *kills* you, to feel so alive out there on a battlefield somewhere, or in a corporate environment where it's quite clear that you're heading for a heart attack, and you don't change your course because you are living in that stream of energy and aliveness. You wind up bargaining your life away for it."

Reading the great philosophers and spiritual teachers, I have come across this advice time and time again. The greatest minds in the history of humankind insist that the costs of denying your heart's desire are far greater than anything that could happen by following it. When my clients overcome their reluctance to know who they are, they release an inner power that transforms their lives. I have seen the beauty of these changes over and over again.

Because the search for meaning is clouded in mystery and the clues are often intangible, I use the following metaphor with many of my clients who want to begin a search for meaning.

A Metaphor: The Grand Plan

Because our world and our lives are so miraculous and each of us is unique, with different genetic mixes, different fingerprints, different gifts, and personalities, it's possible to imagine there must be a reason for our uniqueness, a Grand Plan. Perhaps this Plan has a special place for each of us, and you and I have been designed for a special task within the Plan. Supposing that Plan exists. What is your part in it? What were you designed to do? What's your "job on earth"?

If you feel confused or overwhelmed by life, or if your life seems to have no meaning, no important reason for your existence, consider what your purpose might be in the Plan. Try reading The Planner's mind a little: Imagine—if you were making a Grand Plan, and you bad created the human being that is you, what would you have created that person for? It's an interesting puzzle, and the clues are in your unique characteristics. Are you a good listener? Then maybe counseling is your intended "job." Are you a mathematical whiz? A musician? An artist? Can you make people laugh? All of these talents can be used in unique ways to make the world a little better. For example, if you like to make people laugh and you enjoy elderly people, perhaps entertaining, volunteering, or working in a senior citizens' center is your special place. Or if you are a survivor of abuse or illness, perhaps your "job" lies in helping others survive.

Many of my clients have found it useful to ponder and solve this riddle. The clues and hints are subtle, but they exist. The secret to your life's purpose is hidden in your heart's desire. Discover that, and you discover meaning, joy, and purpose. There is a Plan, and you fit within it. No one has been omitted, every small link fits. As you discover your secret mission and join the rhythm of the Intelligent Plan, life begins to run itself, doubt fades, and joy becomes a more frequent companion. Try listening to your heart and to the obvious things about you, and you'll find it works.

Dr. Campbell suggests:

> "You must have a room, or a certain hour or so a day, where you
> don't know what was in the newspapers that morning, you don't

know who your friends are, you don't know what you owe anybody, you don't know what anybody owes to you. This is a place where you can simply experience and bring forth what you are and what you might be. This is the place of creative incubation. At first, you may find that nothing happens there. But if you have a sacred place and use it, something eventually will happen.. .Where is your bliss station? You have to try to find it. Get a phonograph and put on the music that you really love, even if it's corny music that nobody else respects. Or get the book you like to read. In your sacred place you get the "thou" feeling of life. ..for the whole world. I even have a superstition that has grown on me as a result.. .that if you do follow your bliss you put yourself on a kind of track that has been there all the while, waiting for you, and the life that you ought to be living is the one you are living. When you can see that, you begin to meet people who are in the field of your bliss, and they open the doors to you. I say, follow your bliss and don't be afraid, and doors will open where you didn't know they were going to be."

Writing Your Constitution

In order to support your search for meaning in your life, you can also follow the suggestion of spiritual teacher Jason Lotterhand, author of *Thursday Night Tarot,* and write a "constitution" for yourself. He writes:

> The value of this exercise is that it helps clarify what our objectives are and thereby gives some point to our lives. By this act we accept spiritual responsibility for ourselves.. .When we grow up, spiritually speaking.. .We begin to think in terms of what *we* want to do with our life and energies.. .You may feel that you don't know enough to constitute yourself, or that you have to make compromises with the world. But you have to start *somewhere,* and our teachers tell us that the best place to start is with a piece of paper and a pen. Just as the fathers of the United States sat down and wrote a constitution— which was ridiculous at the time, because they didn't even have a country—you should sit down and write the story of the marvelous creature you're going to develop into. It might be considered an act of faith by some...When you muster all your powers and faculties together—which is what you do when you write your constitution— they become available to you in a practical way so that you can manipulate them in the direction of your heart's desire...
> Concentrate on what you would like to be or what you think you

are. Try **to** express what you want to have happen for yourself...The whole idea is that you are the only one who can figure out what you would like to be or what you really are. You say, "Well, I think that I am thus and so." Put that down on a piece of paper. Review it every day. See if it works. Then if you don't like it, amend it as much as your want.

As time goes on, you'll find that by some strange magic, you come to a decision as to what kind of person you really are, what you really want for yourself, and so on. In other words, you *define yourself to yourself* This is important because the only one you can live with—day in and day out, year in and year out, *forever—is* your True Self. Nothing else will do. My definition of you will not do. Your best friend's definition will not do. The only one to hit the mark is the one you create for yourself. Writing your constitution makes you concentrate on the all-important question, "Who am I?"

Details are amendments. They will change, but I think you'll find that the basic note around which you want to build your life will stay much the same from beginning to end. Finally, you can tell that you have succeeded in this process when you don't want to amend your constitution any more. You are pleased with it. If you can stand your constitution for, say, a year, you're in business. When you get up in the morning you won't have to *read* your constitution because you will have *learned* it. You look at it and you say, " It's okay. I like it! I like me! I can define myself in understandable terms to myself."

Writing this constitution, as Mr. Lotterhand presents it, is a work in progress—you keep working with it until it feels right to you. This is a basic truth about you and your life. Each of us is *always* in process, never completely finished. To seek to live your life according to a purpose is to commit to lifelong learning and self-development.

Whichever method of searching you choose, you are seeking to get acquainted with your heart's desire and to learn to find and follow your bliss, and the result will be a life full of meaning. Make a resolution to surrender, to slow down and find out what is inside, straining to get out, longing to make contact with you. Make a "sacred space" for yourself, and spend a little time in it, at first reading or listening to music and little by little listening to your heart. It will likely change your life, as it has so many others.

Few people envision a successful life for themselves without including a successful intimate relationship as a major component. So, let's consider how to create a healthy relationship when your early experience might be growing up in the midst of dysfunction.

Defining Love

When your history includes family problems, the idea of finding a partner with whom you can create a healthy relationship might be discouraging and overwhelming. You may have tried looking, and failed, and now you're discouraged and frustrated, or you may be so intimidated by the idea of even trying that you give up before you begin.

No matter what your past experience has been, making a relationship work is not as difficult as you may think. As I discussed earlier, most people have a tendency to love in reactive and responsive ways—that is, to just respond to whatever happens, without thinking about what it means. In business, you would not just respond without thinking and let your emotional reactions rule your intellect, because we tend to think through our actions and decisions when they involve work or money. But, in love, it's common to act on feelings, without thinking. That doesn't work any better in your love life than it would in your career.

Here are some simple steps to follow that will increase your chances of success, no matter who you are or whom you are seeking. You may want to set aside a notebook just for these exercises and to record your progress.

EXERCISE

Receiving Love

Each of us has a different need for giving and receiving love. To create the kind of relationship you really want, you need to understand your personal definition of love. For single people, this step is great to do on a lonely evening. It helps counteract your loneliness, and it fills time. Couples can use these exercises as a basis for discussion.

Give yourself some uninterrupted time in your sacred space and think back over your life from childhood to today. Call up all the times you felt loved. Even if you had a miserable childhood, there will be loving moments. Every kindness shown by friends, teachers, grandparents, extended family, neighbors, and so on counts. You can even use scenes from books, movies, and television to imagine words, actions, and events that symbolize love to you. Take the time to do this thoroughly. Fantasies and reminiscences become richer when you stay with them for a while. When you have a collection of scenes, words, and gestures that symbolize love to you, write them down in list form.

Your list might look something like this:

Love is:

> Being understood

> Physical affection (hugs, a gentle touch)

> Great sex

> Time spent with someone special

> Sentimental gifts

> Eye-to-eye contact

- ➢ A surprise party

- ➢ Quiet talks

- ➢ The whole family together at dinner

- ➢ Phone calls for no special reason

- ➢ A card game with silly jokes and laughter

- ➢ Knowing when to leave me alone and when to offer comfort

- ➢ An energetic game of tag, hide-and-seek, or touch football

You can continue to add to this, and let it grow. The more you know about what feels loving to you, the easier it will be to recognize when you see it and to negotiate and work it out with someone else.

EXERCISE

Giving Love

At another time, repeat the previous exercise to find out times and situations when you felt *loving*. Don't be surprised if this varies a bit from feeling loved. Giving and receiving are often different. Go through memories, movies, and other examples and create a list as you did in the previous exercise. Again, give these memories enough time to form.

Making these two lists should give you a clearer picture of love, as you experience it. Once you have the two lists, review them, and contrast these characteristics with the kind of relationships you have been having. How well do they match up?

EXERCISE

Partner Preferences

Now that you're prepared with knowledge of the kind of love you're looking for, you need to find someone who complements or contrasts with you in the way that works best. For example, if you like talking, do you want a partner who is as verbal as you are, or would someone who's a good listener be a good match? If a sexual connection is of primary importance, do you want someone who is more assertive (that is, initiates sex, takes the lead, is very giving), someone who is more receptive (waits for you to initiate, is very accepting, wants to please you), or someone about the same as you? The next section develops this theme further.

EXERCISE

Essential Qualities

"Before you start your search," recommends "Ask Isadora" columnist Isadora Alman, in her "Sweetie Search" workshop, "it helps to have some perspective on where you've been: to learn from your successful as well as your not-so-successful encounters." She recommends making a list of 10 qualities that are essential to you in an intimate friend, such as a sense of humor, intelligence, good health, honesty, success, and so on. Write your list down the center of the page and then, on the left side, rate each quality in order of importance, from 1 (most important) to 10 (least important). Then, on the right side, rate yourself in each quality, also from 1 to 10. When you have the columns finished, you have a simple way to see how similar or different you would like your partner to be. Perhaps you consider success important in a partner and gave it a 1, but when you look at your own characteristics, success only rates a 5.

Whether your ratings come out very similar on both sides or are very different, it's okay. What's important is knowing that you want a love who is very similar or very different.

EXERCISE

Review the Past

To explore your inner secrets about what you want, you can examine your past adult love relationships in terms of what you liked and didn't like, what worked for you and what didn't. By analyzing each prior relationship, you can avoid repeating old mistakes, and improve on your prior successes.

Think back through past friends and lovers, and see if the kind of love you shared with them matched your giving and receiving lists. You may find that people in your past matched in some things and not in others. Keep in mind that you're doing this to get clearer on the aspects of love you've been unaware of—the ones that might be confusing your efforts to find a good match.

To review past relationships, choose the ones most significant to you, and list each one on a separate piece of paper. On the left, put the heading, "Positive," and on the right, "Negative." Then list in the left column the things that worked well about your connection with that person, and in the right column what did not work.

When you have done this for each relationship, review the results, and summarize. Having done this, you should be getting more clear on the kind of interaction you want, and the difference between what you settled for in the past, and what would really work. You can create a composite of the kind of person you'd really like as a partner by combining traits of several previous partners and eliminating the undesirable traits.

Awareness Helps You Choose

These steps may seem simplistic when you first read them, but it is not as easy as it looks. In my therapy practice, I find that few people have thought deeply what kind of personality they are, what they want, why they want it, and what kind of person would match that list. We often tend to avoid knowing what we really want or really like, because we're afraid it's not okay or not possible to find.

Knowing how you like to give and receive love helps you:

> ➢ Recognize the right kind of partner when you meet him or her.

> ➢ Express clearly what your wants are so your partner can understand.

> ➢ Know where to look for the proper kind of person.

> ➢ Redefine your idea of a relationship from what the culture says to what would actually work for you.

> ➢ Write a personal ad that accurately reflects who you are and the kind of person you're looking for.

When you explore and analyze what love means to you in all these ways, you will be more successful, because you know what you're looking for, you understand what love means to you, and you can communicate to a partner or potential partner what you know about love.

Power in Relationships
When we think of intimate relationships, we usually think of love, but power is also a tremendously important component. In relationships, we can learn skills that give us more power to get our needs met, and we can gain understanding that gives us more power to get along with the other people involved. There are three main types of power in relationships:

1. The Power of Personal Space.

2. The Power of Privacy.

3. The Power of Self-Control.

The Power of Personal Space

Personal space is difficult to describe. It is the emotional and physical room you need to be comfortable. We all know when we don't have enough—when we feel crowded, pressured, and uncomfortable. Intimacy can be compared to food and shelter, because we need it as much. But just as with food and shelter, no one needs it all the time, and some people need more than others. As human beings, we have both a need to belong and a need to be unique. We want to be accepted, to belong, and we also want to be special and recognized as different. These needs often appear to conflict as we search for the balance point between them.

Pressure for Intimacy

It's often surprising to realize that the intimacy that comes with a relationship can be a problem. One or more partners in a relationship will often feel stress or pressure about too much closeness—not enough separateness. If you feel you have to "cater to" or "be nice to" your partner all the time, and put aside what you really want to do (your spouse insists on talking about the relationship when you'd rather just zone out in front of the TV, for example), you'll feel resentful and want to get away from your partner and the related stress.

This problem arises because many of us have hidden "rules" or beliefs about relationships. That is, once we find someone we want to be close to, we feel that we shouldn't ever want to pull away. So, to protect our personal space, we put up unconscious barriers, behaviors and responses that communicate to others: "Go away" or "Don't get too close." Behaving this way, of course, can hurt your partner's feelings and create big problems in the relationship. For example, if you pull away and become quiet or cold, and your partner feels pushed away, doesn't understand it, and panics, then he or she may insist on being reassured by demanding more closeness. This will make your need for space more acute, and you'll pull away further, and your partner will become more demanding. This whole process can lead to struggling, hurt feelings, and anger—and you may not even understand what you're fighting about.

Individual Needs for Personal Space

Your own need for personal space may be a lot different than your partner's, your child's, or others you know, and your partner's personal space can be a lot different from some other partner's needs. For example, eldest or only children usually want more personal space and are more comfortable alone than middle or youngest children or children from big families. This is because eldest/only children are accustomed to spending more time alone than children with lots of siblings.

If you were born in a family whose style was very formal, or a culture, such as the Chinese, who have a great deal of respect for each other's space (though they often live very close together), then you'll be horrified at the idea of people (even an intimate partner) prying into your personal things, reading your diary, trying on your clothes, asking too many questions, or wanting a lot of attention. If, instead, you grew up in a close, very informal family, who had a lot of group activities and interactions, you might be quite comfortable with your spouse being very present, asking lots of questions, and wanting to share everything with you.

No Right or Wrong

Whatever amount of closeness or distance is comfortable for you, even if it's different from your partner's preference, is okay. There is no right or wrong amount of personal space. The problems that arise are created by the partners not recognizing it is natural and normal to be different in personal space requirements. If one of you thinks there's a "rule" about how close a couple should be or how much privacy one should have, and the two of you differ, then struggles can arise. Understanding your own need for personal space can greatly ease, and even eliminate, this problem. For example, if you are able to explain your needs for space and privacy and to understand your partner's early in a new relationship, the two of you have a much better chance of working out agreements that allow you to meet both partners' needs.

The Personal Space Solution

If your relationship is already established and personal space differences are creating problems, they can be fixed through understanding and communication. There are many creative ways to meet different needs, and by acknowledging and meeting everyone's needs your relationships will be strengthened. For example:

> ➢ If your partner needs more alone-time than you do, you can go out for dinner with friends one or two nights a week, while your partner stays home.

> ➢ If your partner wants to discuss the relationship a lot, and you don't like to, you can agree to half-hour discussions of the relationship once a week, which will honor your partner's need for discussion and provides a limit you can manage.

> ➢ If you want lots of friends and family around, and your partner is uncomfortable with groups, you can negotiate to spend some time alone with your family or have your family over when your partner isn't home. Or you can even be in one room with everyone while your partner cooks, barbecues, or makes the drinks and keeps some distance.

Accepting that you and the others you are close to may have differing needs for personal space, learning to identify your own needs and to communicate them, and finding out about others' needs, gives you the information that makes it possible to use the power of personal space to help, rather than hurt, your relationships.

The Power of Privacy

Privacy is your personal power to determine your own internal boundaries and how much of yourself you will share with others. Your private thoughts, your feelings, your personal correspondence, your sexuality, even bathroom time and your clothing are all areas in which you may have different comfort levels than other people. As with personal space, people have differing needs for privacy because of past history. For example, if you grew up with many siblings or a close extended family, which valued sharing, your needs for personal privacy are not nearly as great as someone who grew up as an only child or in an emotionally distant family. As with personal space, respect for privacy and emotional reticence are also highly valued in certain families and cultures.

A Matter of Style

These differences are matters of style, not of right or wrong. Either style, carried to extremes, can become dysfunctional, as when warmth, closeness, and interest become overbearing and smothering—or, on the other hand, when respect for privacy and emotional reticence become cold and stifling.

Knowing how to move between the two modes, and having a choice of when and with whom to use each one, is one of the skills that make the difference between relationships that work and people who are in constant conflict.

Different Strokes

We all have different categories of people in our lives. There are family members, friends, coworkers, colleagues, and acquaintances. And within each of these categories, there are levels of closeness. In your family, for example, you may feel closer and more comfortable with one sister or cousin than you are with another. Or in your circle of friends, some may be much more reliable and warm than others. Even in business, some colleagues may be true friends, whereas others are more distant.

The differences in these relationships determine how much distance or closeness will work in them. Knowing how to exercise your power of privacy will make a big difference.

Circles of Intimacy

To create a mental picture of how the various kinds of intimacy exist in your life, you can imagine your relationships as organized into a series of concentric circles, with you in the center of all of them.

The Center Circle: Intimacy

The people you consider most important to you, who are your closest friends and family, fill the center circle, the smallest one. The circle is small because relatively few people meet the requirements to get into the "inner circle." It is reserved for those who are special—your closest friends, your spouse or partner, and your family.

The Second Circle: Warm friendship

The circle just outside that one, the second circle, is for warm friends and family members whom you like, but perhaps do not know well enough to trust completely or who have some characteristics that make being closer impossible. This can be true for people you like a lot, but who are far away or who can't be trusted to keep commitments or to respond when you need them.

The Third Circle: Friendly connections

This circle is for people you know and like but don't yet know well enough to consider them warm friends. These people may be friends of your friends or family members, or other people you like and enjoy spending time with, but with whom you have not yet made an individual connection. Some of these acquaintances may very well move on into your second circle after some time and experience, although others may drift away.

The Fourth Circle: Circumstantial friends

These people may be neighbors, coworkers, other parents in your child's preschool, or people who are fun to talk to while you work out at the gym, but aren't much closer in your personal life. These people are friendly and convenient for doing certain things together (for example, a coworker with whom you have lunch) but if the circumstances change (you change jobs or move away), the friendships don't last. Once in a while, a circumstantial friend becomes a personal friend and moves into the third circle, or even closer.

The Fifth Circle: Acquaintances

This final circle is for people you've recently met and haven't had a chance to screen for more intimate circles, friends of friends, or other people you hardly know, but consider friendly. You may get to know some of these people better as time goes on.

Being Selective

Each of these circles calls for a different level of privacy. If you have carefully considered who to allow into the innermost circle, for example, it will contain the people with whom you are the most comfortable being intimate. These are the people with whom you share your personal thoughts, your secrets, your sexuality, and your living space (just how close you get depends on your personal preferences and on how considerate and caring they are).

With each successive circle, the level of intimacy and sharing of your private self-diminishes. A new work colleague in the outermost circle, for example, will probably know only general information about you and very little about your personal life.

Making the Choice

Once you understand the different levels involved, the next requirement for optimal use of the power of intimacy in your life is to understand yourself. By taking a personal inventory of your preferences and style, you can pretty quickly discover just how much closeness or privacy you need.

EXERCISE

Intimacy Inventory

Ask yourself the following questions:

1. Do I like to be with one person at a time, or do I prefer a group?

2. Do I prefer to be with other people or alone?

3. If someone else borrowed my clothing, would it feel good, like sharing, or intrusive, as if he or she were taking advantage of me?

4. Would I rather talk to someone, listen to him or her, or read to myself?

Asking yourself questions of this nature will help you get in touch with how much privacy or closeness you need. Once you know your personal privacy needs, you'll be much more aware of when the intimacy level in your various relationships feels good and when it doesn't.

To learn about the intimacy needs of other people you know, observe them carefully:

> ➢ Who sits or stands closer to you at a party, and who keeps some distance?

> ➢ Who shares a lot of personal information, and who keeps personal details secret?

> ➢ Who is curious about you? Who never asks?

> ➢ Who tends to touch people on the shoulder or arm? Who hugs? Who never touches except for a handshake?

> ➢ Of your coworkers, who is all business? Who likes to have friendly chats?

> ➢ Do you know of siblings who share clothing and are always talking about feelings? Do you know other siblings who hardly talk?

All these details are clues to the privacy needs of the people around you. If you pay attention, people will demonstrate their tolerance level for intimacy. Once you understand your own needs for privacy, and the difference between your needs and the needs of others, you will find that you can work out privacy issues much more easily in all your relationships. Knowing the power of privacy will help you improve all your relationships.

The Power of Self-Control

Most people would like to be able to control others—to cause someone to love them, or to make someone behave better, or to get them to leave them alone. Unfortunately, it is impossible for any of us to truly control another person. What many people have a tendency to forget is that we have *total* power to control ourselves and that, if we use this power effectively, we can influence others quite a bit.

Response

In relationships, most of the interactions are responses. That is, you do something (stimulus), I respond to what you do (response); you respond to my response, I respond to your response; you respond to my counter-response, and so on. There are a few original actions or statements, and all the rest are reactions. This means that, if you control your actions and your responses, you control a great deal of the relationship. Twill respond according to what you do.

For a simple illustration of this, imagine I walk into the room, see you, and say, in a disgusted tone of voice, "Oh. It's you," sounding not very pleased to see you. How would you feel, and how would the rest of our interaction go?

Now, imagine that I walk into the room, see you, and say, "How nice to see you!" in a really pleased tone, with a big smile. How would you feel then, and how would our interaction go?

Obviously, we are much more likely to have an easy, comfortable time with each other in the second example, because my initial action (being glad to see you) set up a better series of responses, obviously, than if I were not glad to see you.

This simple metaphor illustrates a profound fact. Anyone who is willing to do the work necessary to control his or her emotions, reactions, and responses can control the vast majority of a relationship. We often don't realize how much our reactions contribute to a partner's behavior.

If your partner is angry, for example, and begins to yell, but you remain calm and quiet and just remain there, obviously listening but not reacting, your partner will "run out of steam" and stop yelling quite quickly, because it feels very uncomfortable to yell if no one is yelling back.

If you take care to speak to your partner and your family in positive, loving ways and address them directly with kindness, you'll find that very soon they will all begin to be more kind and considerate of you. However, if you yell and nag at your children to "be nice," they are more likely to yell, or be resentful and sullen, than to be considerate.

Learning Self-Control

Maintaining this type of attitude, however, is a lot easier to describe than it is to do. Self-control is not easy. In the face of your partner's actions, it's difficult not to react. Learning to stop and think, to respond *thoughtfully* and *carefully* rather than quickly and automatically, is hard. However, mastering self-control, no matter how difficult, is always worthwhile, because it makes every moment of your life easier.

Self-control begins with self-awareness. If you already *know* what pushes your buttons, you will be less reactive to it. If you can tell when you're stressed, you can be more cautious at those times. If you know that you and your partner tend to fight about the same things, over and over, you can learn to exercise more self-control when those things are discussed and react differently to avoid fighting.

It is not necessary to keep tight self-control all the time. If you and your partner are relaxing and having fun, you can most likely respond spontaneously and be fine. But if you're in a tense situation, extra tired, frustrated, stressed, or talking about a sensitive subject, thinking about your response in advance will make the whole interaction work a lot better.

For example, if the two of you are just relaxing on a weekend, you can probably feel free to tease your partner, joke around, and be playful. But if you're talking about financial problems or jealousy, your responses need to be much more carefully considered.

Choosing Your Response

Each of us has his or her own sphere of influence, our own private space, which we can picture as a physical boundary surrounding us, akin to the invisible "glass wall" mimes often pretend to be trapped behind. All other people and events are outside this boundary, but visible and accessible through it. You can send messages with words and deeds (and perhaps even thoughts and subtle body and facial movements) through this boundary, and others can send theirs in to you. You have little control over what people choose to send toward you and total control over what you choose to send out. The control you *do* have over what people send into your world consists in how you *receive* it and *respond to* it.

For example, if your spouse or your boss sends you some crabbiness, you can't change the fact that it's been sent your way. Perhaps there is some other problem (having nothing to do with you) that accounts for this bad mood. There is little to be gained from attempting to mind-read or to change the other person's attitude. However, if you remember your own private space and your imaginary wall, you will realize you have many options.

You can choose to believe that the crabbiness was sent to hurt you, or because the other person is your enemy, or because you somehow deserve to be treated that way. Any of these choices will lead to a negative, hurtful response from you, and most likely to an unpleasant interaction.

Or you can choose not to worry about the reason for the crabbiness, and instead assume it is a problem the other person is having, and become helpful. "Are you upset?" "Is there anything I can do to help?" "Will you explain to me what you're upset about?" If you choose to respond this way, you are more likely to have a good, productive talk with the other person.

As long as you remember that your responses will go a long way toward shaping the whole interaction, and eventually your whole relationship; and you take the time to control the way you respond, you will see all your relationships improve dramatically. This kind of self-control is a very powerful tool, when used correctly. By using it wisely, you gain the power to make your relationships, and therefore your life, happier, more successful, and more loving.

Relationships Are for Learning

Especially if you grew up in a dysfunctional family, you may have a lot to learn from love. Understanding and accepting that your intimate relationship will stretch you and cause you to grow will help you create more intimacy and a better sense of partnership.

We are all quite practiced in taking courses. When we sign up for an algebra course, for example, we know what we face: 10 (or so) weeks of learning new material and homework assignments consisting of more and more complex problems based on the material we have learned. We may grumble about the homework load or complain about the teacher, but we never think we've been given the problems because we are bad people. The problems are a natural facet of the educational process.

Life, too, is a classroom with many classes. The signing-up process has become rather subtle and mysterious, so we have a tendency to forget we're in an educational situation. As one of the learning opportunities in life, relationships can perhaps teach us the most. By keeping in mind that you're a student, and that problems are for learning, you'll find your relationships are much easier, growth is faster, and intimacy makes more sense.

To approach your relationships as courses in personal growth, begin by reevaluating the purpose of your relationships. Use them as a training ground. Assume there will be a lot to learn, and lots of problems, which increase in complexity as you gain in knowledge, to solve. Never, ever do the problems indicate that you deserve punishment or that you did something bad. They only show that you have something to learn, and they even give you the means to learn it. A problem does not exist without a valuable lesson attached.

Just as in school, if you do not understand the lesson and solve the problem, you will keep getting it back in altered forms, until you do understand. This is *not* to give you a hard time, but to teach you what you need to know to live a fuller, more loving life.

Doing Your Homework

When problems arise, stop a moment and think before you react with outrage and hurt. Say to yourself, "What was I given this problem for? What can I learn from this? What do I need to know to solve it?" View the problem as a homework assignment, and figure out what it has been designed to teach you.

For example, perhaps your partner is not giving you enough attention. Perhaps this situation has happened before, with this partner and with others. You merely want a kind word, a loving touch; it doesn't seem too much to ask. Yet, this partner and earlier partners, too, seem to find it impossible. What could you possibly learn from this problem?

Perhaps a shortage of attention means you need to learn more about networking, having a circle of friends you can rely on so that your primary relationship is not under the strain and stress of having to meet *all* your needs. When your partner is preoccupied with work problems, illness, or other absorbing facets of life, you can still have many sources of affection and attention.

Learning to Love Yourself

Often a lack of attention means you need to learn the great satisfaction of being able to give attention to *yourself.* When you are unable to love yourself satisfactorily, other people feel a sense of despair about loving you. A lack of self-love makes a person feel like a bottomless pit into which others can pour all their love and not be able to fill it. Frustrated, they give up trying. Learning the lesson of self-love eliminates the problem. It is easy to be successful in loving a person who knows self-love—and everyone loves to be successful.

A deficit of attention might mean you need to learn the art of appreciation, noticing the attention you are given, however slight it may seem. That which is appreciated grows and grows. Again people quickly tire of giving that goes unnoticed. A little appreciation of what is right is a lot more attractive and effective than complaining about what is wrong. Many of the exercises in this book are about learning what you can from your relationships with others.

There are many other examples of the knowledge to be gained from problem-solving this one attention issue. The more carefully and conscientiously you approach your homework, the more you will benefit in increased love and joy.

The Basic Lesson

The most important step you can take toward making your relationship a course in personal growth is to decide that everyone close to you is a friend who is assisting you in your major task of learning. Each of these friends also has lessons to learn, with your help. You can regard all your friends and family as a mutual helping, learning, growing group. Problems and struggles are mutual learning opportunities.

In the midst of a problem, try saying, "I don't know what this is all about, but I know we are friends, and we both have something to learn from this, and I'd like to find out what it is," and see if the atmosphere changes.

Healing Hurts

Healing hurt feelings is another art that can be learned in intimate relationships. Human beings are imperfect and clumsy; we often stumble and hurt each other. The closer we get, the more likely we are to bruise each other emotionally. It's almost guaranteed that your feelings will be hurt in an intimate relationship. With practice, you can learn to heal yourself individually and you and your partner can work together, to heal each other. Whenever you are hurt or upset in a relationship situation, use the exercises in self-awareness you learned to track your pain, discover its source, and get as clear as you can about it. Were you really hurt because your partner ignored you at the party, or is it really because communication has not been good for the past week, and the party was an easy target for your blame? Find out if your hurt comes from where you first thought or if it's possibly an old hurt from another relationship, or from childhood. Once you understand your hurt feelings, share them gently with your partner—no accusations—just a statement of your experience.

If you get agreement, then quite often a simple talk can point out the differences between then and now. Sometimes sharing your clarity becomes the healing. After sharing and talking, figure out a way to protect yourself next time. You'll find that as soon as you know how to protect yourself, all the hurt and anger fade quickly.

A Guide for Your Journey

Most education processes require a teacher, or at least a mentor. Intimacy is a fine art for which we are largely untrained, and many of the role models and guidelines in our society are highly toxic and negative. If you feel stuck in your life or your relationships, don't hesitate to find a teacher, a therapist or other source of information to use as a guide. Books, classes, and workshops can also be very helpful. In addition, there are many wonderful guides and counselors around to help you. Get help in solving problems before they become too large. You deserve to have help with anything that feels difficult or unsolvable. Mastery of any art, inducing intimacy, usually benefits from a good teacher.

When you sign up for your course in personal growth, it's a lifetime study. Have fun with it. Love and joy are the goals; you can reach them if you do your work well and graduate *magna cum laude*. This final exercise will help you turn the page to your new future.

FINAL EXERCISE

Leaving Childhood

Part 1: Sit quietly for a moment and imagine that you're leaving your childhood today. This is a ceremonial occasion, and you're packing your bag. Consider the aspects of childhood, both tangible (material) and intangible (qualities of life, feelings, and so on). Then think about the following questions:

> ➢ What would you take?

> ➢ What would you like to leave behind?

> ➢ Are there any surprises?

> ➢ What past hassles would you like to avoid in the future?

> ➢ What past peaks would you like to re-create?

Part 2: Now consider your previous relationship experiences and ask:
> ➢ How much childhood baggage did you take with you into your past relationships?

> ➢ How much of it was helpful?

> ➢ How much was a hindrance?

> ➢ What about your previous partners' baggage?

As you prepare to leave your childhood baggage behind, taking only what is really valuable to you, look back one more time and say goodbye to the leftovers and family dysfunction of your childhood, then turn toward your future, take a deep breath, and step forward into your new life—a life you will create as you want it to be.

Celebrate your life, and enjoy every minute of it.

Bibliography

AScribe Newswire. "Children From 'Risky Families' Suffer Serious Long-Term Health Consequences, UCLA Scientists Report." Los Angeles, Calif.: March 21.

Bradshaw, John. *Bradshaw on the Family.* Deerfield Beach, Calif.: Health Communications, 1988.

Campbell, Joseph, with Bill Moyers. *The Power of Myth.* New York: Doubleday, 1988.

Galvin, Kathleen. "Multigenerational Transmission of Communication Patterns." Northwestern University Website, 2000.

Groder, Martin M.D. "All About Change." *Bottom Line Persona.* May *15,* 1996.

Janov, Dr. Arthur. *The Biology of Love.* New York: Promethius Books, 2000.

Lotterhand, Jason C. *Thursday Night Tarot.* North Hollywood, Calif.: Newcastle, 1989.

Phillips, Robert, M.D., monograph, "Structural Symbiotic Systems." Chapel Hill, N.C.: August *1975.*

Prochaska, James and John Norcross. *Changing for Good.* New York: Avon, 2000.

Repetti, Rena. *Psychological Bulletin.* March 2002.

Roberts, Denton, M.D., LMFT. *Able and Equal.* Culver City, Calif.: Human Esteem Publishing, 1984.

Satir, Virginia. *Peoplemaking.* Palo Alto, Calif.: Science & Behavior Books, 1972.

Shonkoff, Jack P. and Deborah A. Phillips, Eds. *From Neurons to Neighborhoods.* Washington, D.C.: National Academy Press (National Research Council, Institute of Medicine).

Siegel, Bernie, M.D. *Peace, Love and Healing.* New York: Harper & Row, 1989.

Sinetar, Marsha. *Ordinary People as Monks and Mystics.* Mahwah, N.J.: Paulist Press, 1986.

Szasz, Thomas, Ph.D. *Heresies.* New York: Anchor Books, 1976.

Travers, P.L. "The Unsleeping Eye: A Fairy Tale" *Parabola, The Witness, Vol. 11, No. 1.* Winter 1982.

Tessina, Tina, Ph.D. *The Real]3th Step.* Franklin Lakes, N.J.: New Page Books, 2002.

The 10 Smartest Decisions A Woman Can Make Before 40. Deerfield Beach, Calif.: Health Communications, 1998.

Other Books by the Author

The Ten Smartest Decisions a Woman Can Make After Forty (Muffinhaven, 2014)
Love Styles: How To Celebrate Your Differences (Muffinhaven, 2011)
The Commuter Marriage: Keep Your Relationship Close While You're Far Apart (Adams Media, 2008)
Money, Sex and Kids: Stop Fighting about the Three Things That Can Ruin Your Marriage (Adams Media, 2008)
The Real 13th Step: Discovering Confidence, Self-reliance, and Independence Beyond the Twelve-Step Programs Revised 2nd Edition (New Page Books, 2001)
The Unofficial Guide to Dating Again (Macmilan/IDG, NY 1999)
Gay Relationships: How To Find Them, How To Improve Them, How To Make Them Last (Tarcher, 1989)

with Riley K. Smith
How to Be a Couple and Still Be Free, 3rd Edition (New Page Books, 2002)
True Partners (J.P. Tarcher, 1992)
Equal Partners (Hodder and Stoughton, London 1994),

with Elizabeth Friar Williams
The 10 Smartest Decisions A Woman Can Make Before 40 (HCI, Deerfield Beach, 1998)

Chapter Heading Quote Sources

All quotes from Frank, Leonard Roy. *Quotationeiy* (Random House, 2001).

Introduction: Weitzman, Chaim (1874—1952).

Chapter 1: Forbes, Malcolm S. "Passing Parade." *The Sayings of Chairman Malcolm: The Capitalist's Handbook* (1978).

Chapter 2: Joubert, Joseph *Pensees* (1754—1824), tr. Henry Atwell 1877.

Chapter 3: Wordsworth, William (1770—1 850). "My Heart Leaps Up When I Behold" 1807.

Chapter 4: Paul **(A.D.** 1t Century). Romans 7:19.

Chapter 5: Plotinus **(A.D.** 205—270). *The Enneads,* tr. Stephen MacKenna and BS Page, 1952.

Chapter 6: Twain, Mark (1835—1910). *The Tragedy of Pudd'nhead Wilson,* 1894.

Chapter 7: Hoffer, Eric (1902—1983). *Reflections on the Human Condition,* 1973.

Chapter 8: Emerson, Ralph Waldo (1803—1882). "Success" *Society and Solitude,* 1870.

About the Author

Tina B. Tessina, Ph.D. is a licensed psychotherapist in Long Beach, California since 1978 with over 35 years' experience in counseling individuals and couples and author of 13 books in 17 languages, including *The Unofficial Guide to Dating Again*; *Money, Sex and Kids: Stop Fighting About the Three Things That Can Ruin Your Marriage, The Commuter Marriage*, and most recent, *The Ten Smartest Decisions a Woman Can Make After Forty* and *Love Styles: How to Celebrate Your Differences*. She writes the "Dr. Romance" blog, and the "Happiness Tips from Tina" email newsletter.

Dr. Tessina is CRO (Chief Romance Officer) for LoveForever.com, a website designed to strengthen relationships and guide couples through the various stages of their relationship with personalized tips, courses, and online couples counseling. Online, she's known as "Dr. Romance" Dr. Tessina appears frequently on radio, and such TV shows as "Oprah", "Larry King Live" and ABC News.

Dr. Tessina's many years of experience in helping people shows in her writing. Her books are very practical, filled with "reader-friendly" exercises, suggestions, guidelines, and examples. Although they are simply and elegantly written they are deceptively powerful. Each of Dr. Tessina's books draws on the knowledge she has gained in her years of clinical work with individuals and couples. Each book was written as Dr. Tessina discovered a body of information needed by her clients that was not already published. Her books are not mere speculation, but the concrete result of Dr. Tessina's experiences in helping people overcome their resistance, their fears and their emotional wounds.

In addition to her professional work, Dr. Tessina is a trained opera singer and a lyric coloratura. She also writes poetry and song lyrics (her songs have been recorded by several well-known singers, including Helen Reddy), speaks Spanish and some French, and loves ballroom dancing. She lives in Long Beach, California with her husband of 19 years, Richard Sharrard, ballroom instructor and owner of DanceFactoryOnline.com.   Tina and Richard went around the world in 1998 as dance instructors on the Crystal Symphony cruise ship. They spend the little spare time they have traveling, enjoying their vintage California bungalow, gardening, and playing with their two dogs and one cat.

She earned both her B.A. and M.A. at The Lindenwood Colleges, St. Charles, Missouri (1977), and her Ph.D. at Pacific Western University, Los Angeles (1987). She is a Diplomate of the American Psychotherapy Association and a Certified Domestic Violence Counselor.

Connect with Dr. Tessina online:

http://www.tinatessina.com

Dr. Romance Blog: http://drromance.typepad.com

Twitter.com/tinatessina

Twitter.com/LoveForever

Facebook.com/TinaTessina

Facebook.com/LoveForever

DrRomance@loveforever.com

https://www.facebook.com/DrRomanceBlog

http://www.LoveForever.com

Made in the USA
San Bernardino, CA
15 March 2019